The Making of a Confederate

New Narratives in American History

Series Editors
James West Davidson
Michael B. Stoff

Richard Godbeer   *Escaping Salem: The Other Witch Hunt of 1692*

James E. Crisp   *Sleuthing the Alamo: Davy Crockett's Last Stand and Other Mysteries of the Texas Revolution*

John Hope Franklin and   *In Search of the Promised Land: A Slave Family in the Old South*
Loren Schweninger

Mark H. Lytle   *The Gentle Subversive: Rachel Carson, Silent Spring, and the Rise of the Environmental Movement*

The Making of a Confederate

WALTER LENOIR'S CIVIL WAR

WILLIAM L. BARNEY

OXFORD
UNIVERSITY PRESS

2009

OXFORD
UNIVERSITY PRESS

Oxford University Press, Inc., publishes works that further
Oxford University's objective of excellence
in research, scholarship, and education.

Oxford   New York
Auckland   Cape Town   Dar es Salaam   Hong Kong   Karachi
Kuala Lumpur   Madrid   Melbourne   Mexico City   Nairobi
New Delhi   Shanghai   Taipei   Toronto

With offices in
Argentina   Austria   Brazil   Chile   Czech Republic   France   Greece
Guatemala   Hungary   Italy   Japan   Poland   Portugal   Singapore
South Korea   Switzerland   Thailand   Turkey   Ukraine   Vietnam

Copyright © 2009 by Oxford University Press, Inc.

Published by Oxford University Press, Inc.
198 Madison Avenue, New York, New York 10016

www.oup.com

Oxford is a registered trademark of Oxford University Press

Library of Congress Cataloging-in-Publication Data
Barney, William L.
The making of a Confederate : Walter Lenoir's Civil War / William L. Barney.
p. cm. —(New narratives in American history)
Includes bibliographical references and index.
ISBN-13: 978-0-19-531435-9 (cloth : alk paper)—ISBN-13: 978-0-19-531434-2 (pbk. : alk paper)
1. Lenoir, Walter W.   2. Confederate States of America. Army. North Carolina Infantry
Regiment, 37th.   3. Soldiers—North Carolina—Biography.   4. North Carolina—
History—Civil War, 1861—1865-Biography.   5. United States—History— Civil War,
1861–1865—Biography. 6. Slaveholders—North Carolina—Biography.   7. Landowners—
North Carolina—Biography. 8. Reconstruction (U.S. history 1865—1877)—North
Carolina.   9. Group identity—Confederate States of America—Case Studies.
10. Whites—Race identity—Southern States—Case studies.   I. Title.
E573.537th .B37 2007
973.7'456092—dc22   2007005902
[B]

9 8 7 6 5

Printed in Canada
on acid-free paper

For Elaine, my "Nealy"

CONTENTS

Maps and Illustrations viii
Foreword xi
Acknowledgments xiii
The Lenoir Families xv

PROLOGUE 3

· *One* · DUTIFUL SONS AND A WAVERING
SOUTHERNER 14

· *Two* · CONFEDERATE SOLDIER 46

· *Three* · AGONY AT OX HILL 85

· *Four* · MOUNTAIN FARMER 108

· *Five* · UNRECONSTRUCTED CONFEDERATE 141

· *Six* · LAND PROMOTER AND DREAMER 167

Afterword 203
Recommendations for Further Reading 232
Index 235

Maps and Illustrations

—⁓—

Maps

The Lenoirs' North Carolina in 1860.   12

North Carolina in the 1850s.
    Prior to the Civil War, western North Carolina
    remained isolated from the rest of the state.   28

Walter's journey to Ox Hill.   87

Walter's mountain world.
    After his move to Haywood, Walter rarely left
    the North Carolina mountains. From his homes
    at Crab Orchard and then Shulls Mill, he traveled
    extensively visiting the large landholdings he
    acquired after the war.   109

The railroads come to western Carolina.
    Especially by the 1880s, new rail lines
    opened up the mountain counties to tourists and
    businessmen.   194

ILLUSTRATIONS

Fort Defiance testified to the elite status of the
　　Lenoir family.　　4
The bucolic setting of Fort Defiance overlooking
　　the Yadkin River was suggestive of the estate of
　　an English country gentleman.　　5
As depicted in this 1830 drawing with the
　　family coat of arms, General Lenoir was the
　　personification of patriarchal authority.　　7
Smartly dressed for this 1840 photo, Tom Lenoir
　　faced the world with a boyish openness that
　　left him in a quandary as to the adult role he
　　wanted to assume.　　17
There's no doubting Walter's seriousness and inten-
　　sity of purpose in this photo taken at the time of his
　　graduation from the University of North Carolina.　　18
William's body was discovered in the front yard
　　of Oak Lawn, the Norwoods' home in Lenoir.　　54
This was the scene confronting a burial detail of
　　Union soldiers after the battle of Fair Oaks
　　during the Peninsula Campaign. The crotched
　　sticks had been used to support tents at
　　a Union campsite.　　74
Cedar Mountain looms in the background as Union
　　troops prepare to move against the Confederate lines.　　78
Comparable to Walter's haunting memory of the
　　dead William Weaver is this image of a soldier killed
　　in the Petersburg trenches in the last days of the war.　　82

On the morning of August 31, the day Walter was
    wounded, Pope's army regrouped in Centreville. 88

Walter was wounded while resting behind the
    fence in the foreground of this 1907 view of
    the field where he and his men fought at Ox Hill. 89

Like Walter after the battle at Ox Hill, these
    wounded Union soldiers in Virginia had to wait
    their turn for medical treatment. 90

This Confederate field hospital at Antietam
    was typical of the emergency medical services
    provided for the wounded after a battle. 92

This was the wooden leg Walter favored. 111

Increasing numbers of deserters hid out in
    the mountains of North Carolina. 114

Whether raiding government supplies or
    helping feed deserters among their kinfolk,
    women in the mountains increasingly turned
    against the Confederate war effort. 135

These African Americans registering to vote in
    Asheville in 1867 eagerly took part in a political
    revolution that stamped Reconstruction as
    unacceptably radical for most Southern whites. 174

By the 1880s railroads were carrying tourists to
    new resort hotels in the mountains of western
    North Carolina. 195

Golfers prepare to tee off on the course of the Hot
    Springs Hotel northwest of Asheville. 196

Shown here in 1904, Rufus outlived all his Lenoir
    siblings. 200

Foreword

———

WILLIAM BARNEY'S MARVELOUS TALE, *THE MAKING OF A Confederate*, is likely to catch its readers off guard. Barney is drawn to the question of Southern white identity and its tortuous relationship to that seminal event in its creation, the Civil War. He is well aware of the way Lost Cause proponents have reshaped the war's narrative to forge a white identity shorn of its more troubling aspects. In the eyes of those proponents, the cause that was lost in Southern defeat was the fight for states' rights and the right to secede from the Union. Slavery, the South's "peculiar institution," became a secondary, almost glancing part of their narrative.

The obvious counter to this mythology is to demonstrate, as more than one scholar has, that the leaders of the secession movement boldly and repeatedly insisted at the time that slavery was "the immediate cause of the late rupture," to quote Confederate Vice President Alexander Stephens in March 1861. States' rights was more a political tool than a sacrosanct principle, and Southerners willingly used federal power to override the wishes of Northern states, as when the Fugitive Slave Law employed federal power to force Northerners to protect slavery.

Barney understands these facts, of course, but in exploring the creation of a Southern white identity he has not rounded up the usual fire-eating suspects. Instead, he tells the story of an unstereotypical planter and his extended family. Walter Lenoir was not a low-country nabob who gloried in slavery's positive good or saw the institution as central to his life. He came from the piedmont country of North Carolina and professed to find the slaves he owned almost more of a burden than they were worth. In the late 1850s he remained a Unionist and even considered moving to Minnesota. (His land-hunting expedition up north makes a fascinating counterpoint to a similar search about the same time by a former Tennessee slave, James Thomas, whose journey is profiled in a companion book in this series by John Hope Franklin and Loren Schweninger, *In Search of the Promised Land*.)

When the war came, however, Walter Lenoir and his family threw their support to the Confederacy, and Barney skillfully traces the anguished steps of a soldier who serves, fights, is severely wounded, and ultimately is transformed by the war as he struggles to give meaning to the remainder of his life. The end result is an unorthodox tale of one man's Lost Cause. We discover, with fresh eyes, how Lenoir deals with the patriarchal burdens of family history and grapples with the often troublesome relations with his slaves and with poor white tenants on his lands. It is not the story we were expecting, and as such exhibits what the editors hope is one prime virtue of the Oxford New Narratives in American History: the pleasure of being caught off guard.

James West Davidson
Michael B. Stoff
Series Editors

ACKNOWLEDGMENTS

—∿∿—

T HE MANUSCRIPTS IN THE SOUTHERN HISTORICAL COLLECTION
at the University of North Carolina–Chapel Hill are a researcher's
dream, a point driven home to me as I pieced together Walter
W. Lenoir's story from the documents in the Lenoir Family
Papers. My first thanks are to Tim West and his staff for the high
standards they have maintained in preserving the collection and
adding to it. For ready access to materials and congenial working conditions, the Southern provides all a researcher could ever
hope for. I owe a similar debt to the assistance I received from
the North Carolina Collection at the University of North Caro
lina–Chapel Hill, Perkins Library at Duke University, and the
North Carolina Department of Archives and History in Raleigh.
For helping to shorten the time frame for the research and writing, I'm grateful to the University of North Carolina–Chapel Hill
for a research leave in the fall of 2005.

In addition to numerous colleagues who provided critical
insights as I talked about my project with them, two individuals
deserve special thanks for the painstaking care they took in reading

the manuscript: my wife Elaine and my series editor at Oxford University Press, Jim Davidson. Elaine went over the manuscript word by word and was invaluable in flagging literary gaffes and instances of muddled thinking. She was one of my sharpest and most helpful critics. Jim was a shrewd tutor on the finer points of relating a story with a novelist's attention to narrative flow and telling details. Of all the editors I've worked with over the years, he easily stands as the most helpful. Finally, I would like to thank my students, past and present, for prodding me into thinking of ways to make history come as alive for them as it does for me.

The Lenoir Families

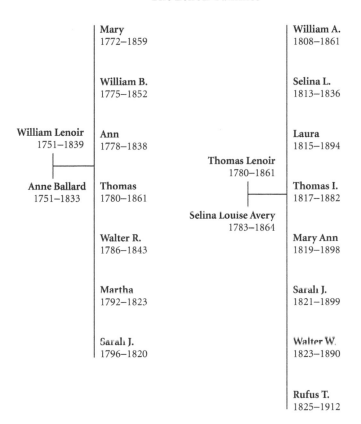

William Lenoir
1751–1839

Anne Ballard
1751–1833

Mary
1772–1859

William B.
1775–1852

Ann
1778–1838

Thomas
1780–1861

Walter R.
1786–1843

Martha
1792–1823

Sarah J.
1796–1820

Thomas Lenoir
1780–1861

Selina Louise Avery
1783–1864

William A.
1808–1861

Selina L.
1813–1836

Laura
1815–1894

Thomas I.
1817–1882

Mary Ann
1819–1898

Sarah J.
1821–1899

Walter W.
1823–1890

Rufus T.
1825–1912

The Making of a Confederate

War, Memory, and Confederate Identity

—∿—

THE CIVIL WAR FORGED A SOUTHERN WHITE IDENTITY THAT has persisted to the present day. For all the advances in racial cooperation that flowed out of the civil rights movement of the 1960s and for all the cultural diversity that accompanied the economic boom celebrated in Atlanta's hosting of the Olympics in 1996, white identity politics remains alive and well in the South. A longing for a South that could have been—*should* have been— shapes much of that identity. Unable to let go of the Confederate past and the belief that hypocritical and power-hungry Yankees unjustly attacked heroic, liberty-loving Southerners and crushed their bid for independence through the sheer weight of their numbers and material resources, many Southern whites continue to find meaning and purpose in their lives by clinging to a romanticized vision of a mythic Southern past.

No Southern writer wrestled more imaginatively or painfully with how the past intrudes into the Southern present or how memories are remembered and recast than William Faulkner.

"The past is never dead. It's not even past," asserted Faulkner. In a memorable passage from his 1948 novel *Intruder in the Dust*, the novelist imagined the longings of Southern boys to undo the results of the Civil War, to turn defeat into victory, by returning to "the instant when it's still not yet two o'clock on that July afternoon in 1863" when Pickett's men were poised for their charge at Gettysburg. A modern observer tempted to dismiss Faulkner's words, written more than fifty years ago, as trite in today's South would do well to ponder the motivations of present-day Confederates who march in the sweat and grime

As Originally Built (from an Oil Painting)

Fort Defiance testified to the elite status of the Lenoir family.
(SOURCE: *North Carolina Collection, Wilson Library, University of North Carolina–Chapel Hill.*)

LANDSCAPE NEAR FORT DEFIANCE IN HAPPY VALLEY. FROM AN OIL PAINTING.

The bucolic setting of Fort Defiance overlooking the Yadkin River was suggestive of the estate of an English country gentleman.
(SOURCE: *North Carolina Collection, Wilson Library, University of North Carolina–Chapel Hill.*)

of their authentic uniforms in reenactments or the passions and contentious politics stirred up in the public display of the Confederate flag.

No one knew better that Gettysburg could not be refought and won than the Southern whites who survived the carnage of that terrible war. They were physically beaten, and they knew it. Out of that physical defeat, however, they forged a spiritual victory, what one Missouri veteran at a Confederate reunion in 1906 termed "a new religion." A blend of Protestant evangelicalism and Southern romanticism, this "new religion" gave meaning to their collective suffering by re-imagining the Old South as a sacred place baptized in the blood of its selfless Christian soldiers who sacrificed their lives against unholy Northern invaders. Here was a faith that by immortalizing the departed filled a void in lives torn apart by the loss of loved ones. Like all religions, it invested cultural symbols and material artifacts with a sacred status. Dutiful worshippers venerated the Confederate flag, specifically the Southern Cross that originally was a battle flag, the tattered gray jacket of the common Johnny Reb, and the song "Dixie" in rituals of commemoration spontaneously organized at first by Confederate widows and then more formally by organizations such as the United Confederate Veterans and the United Daughters of the Confederacy. Robert E. Lee, Thomas J. "Stonewall" Jackson, and Jefferson Davis headed a group of Confederate leaders elevated into the pantheon of Christian sainthood.

Underpinning this sacred image of the South was the mythology of the Lost Cause, a retelling of the history of the slave South and the causes of the Civil War spread by ex-Confederates after the war. For Wade Hampton, a celebrated ex-Confederate cavalry commander, such a retelling was nothing less than the responsibility of all true Southerners. "As it was the duty of every man to devote himself to the service of his country in that great struggle which has ended so disastrously...so, now, when that country is prostrate in the dust,...every patriotic impulse should urge her surviving children to vindicate the great principles for which she fought." The efforts of Hampton and others were so successful that by the 1880s the claims of the Lost Cause dominated not only the Southern white memory of the sectional conflict but also were beginning to shape the Northern memory as well.

Best understood as an effort toward moral rehabilitation, this version of Southern history transformed the tensions and conflict of the Old South into a timeless image of social harmony and genteel grace. Its adherents did not so much erase enslaved African Americans from the story as they caricatured them as the contented, indeed happy, servants of benevolent Christian

As depicted in this 1830 drawing with the family coat of arms, General Lenoir was the personification of patriarchal authority.
(SOURCE: *North Carolina Collection, Wilson Library, University of North Carolina–Chapel Hill.*)

masters who cared for their every need. Led by high-toned men of aristocratic lineage, the so-called Cavaliers, Southern whites valiantly struggled to defend their liberties and way of life from the unceasing assaults of money-grubbing Puritanical Yankees who hypocritically attacked slavery only after they had ceased making money off the institution. When the war came, the South fought only in self-defense and only for the sacred principles of constitutional freedoms and self-government bequeathed to them by their Revolutionary forefathers. United in the holy, legitimate cause of the Confederacy that had nothing to do with the defense of slavery, Southern whites proved themselves worthy of Christian martyrdom as they sacrificed their lives and property on behalf of their independence.

Left out or ignored in this rendering of the Old South and the Confederate experience were the leading secessionists who repeatedly insisted that the South had to leave the Union in order to protect slavery. Nowhere to be found are the white Unionists, the growing bands of deserters from Confederate armies, and the African American slaves who seized every opportunity presented by the war to gain their freedom. As William W. Freehling recently argued in *The South vs. the South*, Southerners, white and black, spent much of the Civil War fighting against each other. Also missing from the accounts of the Lost Cause are the complexity and diversity of late antebellum Southern society, the violence and often brutal discipline that structured the institution of slavery, and the conflicts experienced by many Southern whites as they struggled to reconcile their belief that slavery was morally unjust with their even stronger conviction that emancipation would plunge the South into racial chaos and horror.

One way to pull together and make sense of these missing elements is through a story that opens a window into the nineteenth century South and explores how one Southern white came to identify himself in terms of his Confederate experience. It's a story centered on Walter W. Lenoir, a slaveholding North Carolinian who, despite morally opposing slavery and preparing to move to the free state of Minnesota in 1860, enlisted in the Confederate army and became a fervid Confederate.

Walter Lenoir's South lies outside the South of the popular imagination. It was not a wealthy region of sprawling cotton and sugar plantations but of mixed agriculture and a small minority of slaveholders engaged in a variety of economic activities. Unlike the Lower or Cotton South, which is too often identified with the South as a whole, the dominant political party was not the Democrats committed to the defense of slavery as a positive good and championing states' rights arguments justifying secession from the Union. Instead, across the foothills and mountains of the western North Carolina that Walter knew so well, the politically moderate Whigs were the majority party, and they consistently upheld the value of the Union and looked to economic development within it as the key to the future prosperity of the South.

In the Lower South, where slaves made up close to half of the total population and where nearly two in five white families owned at least one slave, the paramount need to defend slavery was so great that the mere election to the presidency of an anti-slavery Republican was sufficient to trigger a successful secession movement. Citing Lincoln's election as an intolerable threat to slavery, secessionists carried seven states out of the Union stretching from South Carolina to Texas. Delegates from these seven states met in Montgomery, Alabama, in February 1861 and fashioned a new Southern government, the Confederate States of America. Still, eight of the fifteen slave states hung back. In these states, slavery lacked the overwhelming centrality that it had in the Lower South as both an economic investment and a means of racial control. Across the Middle and Upper South, home to two-thirds of the South's white population, voters rejected secession by two-to-one margins in a series of special elections. Everything changed with lightning speed in mid-April 1861 with the fighting that erupted over Fort Sumter and then Lincoln's call on the states for militia troops to put down what he defined as a rebellion against the U.S. government. Almost uniformly denounced in the South as a declaration of war, Lincoln's call for troops converted wavering Unionists into Confederates committed to defending their homes and families against what they saw as an unconscionable invasion.

As revealed by Walter's transformation during the secession crisis from defender of the Union to supporter of the Confederacy, secession was a process that affected Southern whites in different ways at different times and not a spontaneous outpouring of sentiment across the entire South against Northern aggressions, real or perceived. Like many Southerners, Walter's family was ambivalent about secession and going into the war. The pressures of history, as Faulkner understood, shaped and warped and bent the four brothers who got dragged into the cataclysmic conflict. One brother sat out the war; one raised a military company but then, without ever having seen combat, left the army; one committed suicide; and one lost a limb in battle and became a loner, living in isolation for the rest of his life. For him, the past truly was never past and the Cause that was not lost to begin with, became a Lost Cause that was never there in 1861.

For Walter, and a surprisingly large number of his friends and kin, emancipation came as the release from a burden and it was accompanied by something approaching relief. The Union Army, as Walter perceptively noted, would not allow emancipation to explode into a bloodbath costing the lives of Southern whites. While the Union military was acting to stabilize the very social relations it was upending, recently constructed Confederate identities began to unravel. Anti-Confederate sentiment emerged early in the war in western North Carolina. Once the reality of a long, cruel war set in, disaffection spread and became a major problem among both civilians and the soldiers. Tom Norwood, Walter's nephew, informed him in the summer of 1864 that the men in his old regiment, the North Carolina 37th, were "not only tired but sick of the war."

Southern whites reacted to defeat in the Civil War in a variety of ways ranging from depression and self-exile to a willingness to reach an accommodation with the victors. Common to most of these responses, however, was a unifying set of themes: a refusal to acknowledge that they had done anything wrong in bringing on the war; an honoring of their Confederate dead and their sacrifices; a deeply rooted denial that the freed slaves were "ready" for freedom or should be allowed to participate in public life on terms of equality; and a search for a new foundation for a prosperous economy now that slavery had been destroyed. Walter's postwar search for a redemptive meaning to his life speaks to these themes with an intensity and purpose that were nothing less than a strategy for coping with bereavement and a crushing sense of loss. For Walter,

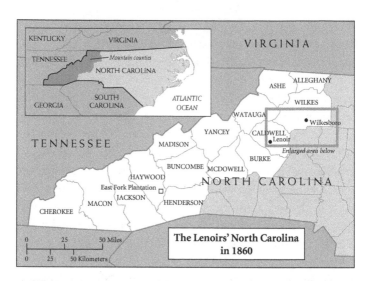

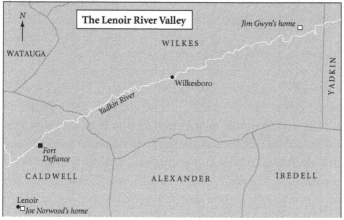

The Lenoirs' North Carolina in 1860.

and many other Confederates, the war had never really ended. All that had changed with the surrender of Confederate armies was the focus of their defense of the South.

What follows then is Walter's story. It is a story that invites the reader to confront the ambiguities and complexities of a South that have been effaced in the haze of the Lost Cause mythology. And from Walter's story, they will learn that an abiding and culturally unifying sense of Southern white identity was a product of defeat in the very Civil War that so many Southerners sought to prevent.

NOTES

For the Faulkner quotes, see William Faulkner, *Requiem for a Nun* (New York: Random House, third printing, 1950), p. 92 and *Intruder in the Dust* (New York: Random House, 1948), p. 194. The Wade Hampton quote can be found in Richard Gray, *Writing the South: Ideas of an American Region* (Baton Rouge: Louisiana State University Press, 1997), p. 76, a work that offers a finely grained account of the ways in which Southern writers have shaped how Southerners imagine and re-imagine their past. Tom Norwood's letter to Walter Lenoir on July 18, 1864, is in the Lenoir Family Papers, Southern Historical Collection, University of North Carolina at Chapel Hill.

The broad themes mentioned in the prologue and the historiography that addresses them are discussed in greater depth in the afterword. A special note can be made here, however, of the myth of the Lost Cause which has loomed so large in how Southern whites remember the Civil War. The essays edited by Gary W. Gallagher and Alan T. Nolan, *The Myth of the Lost Cause and Civil War History* (Bloomington: Indiana University Press, 2000) explore how the Lost Cause falsified the past and, in so doing, assumed a life of its own. For an often humorous but still serious look at those Southern whites who still passionately embrace the Lost Cause, see Tony Horwitz, *Confederates in the Attic: Dispatches from the Unfinished Civil War* (New York: Pantheon Books, 1998).

· One ·

DUTIFUL SONS AND A WAVERING SOUTHERNER

—ᴗᴗᴗ—

FORT DEFIANCE, WALTER LENOIR'S CHILDHOOD HOME, WAS at the emotional center of the South he would come to identify with as his "country" when the Civil War broke out. Until forced to choose between the North or the South, he had been a wavering Southerner torn between his moral reservations over slavery and his obligations as a male heir of a leading North Carolina family. Like his uncles and brothers, he enjoyed the privileges of elite status even as he struggled to break free from the patriarchal authority that conferred that status. Walter's story, then, is inseparable from that of the Lenoir clan, which forged the familial ties of burdens and obligations, support and comfort that infused Walter with a sense of duty that drove his life until the day of his death.

Walter's story thus begins with his grandfather, William Lenoir, the source of the Lenoirs' power and prestige, who built the family house in the early 1790s. Set on a hilltop with a commanding view of the Yadkin River winding through west central North

Carolina, the house was large yet inviting. Occupying the site of an old colonial fort and known as Fort Defiance, it left no doubt as to the wealth and status of its owner, the Revolutionary War hero William Lenoir. The plans for the house came from England, as did the original hardware, the glass, and most of its furnishings. In its sheer size—twenty-eight by forty feet, two stories of four rooms each—it dwarfed the crude, one-room log cabins that were home to most of the Yadkin River valley's white residents in the late eighteenth century. The sixteen windows with paneled shutters, the brick used in the interior construction of the walls, the tongue-and-groove flooring, and the thick roof shingles were all refinements that only the very wealthy could afford. At the center of a villagelike setting that included Lenoir's gristmill, smokehouse, blacksmith shop, and slave quarters, Fort Defiance stamped the Lenoir family as among the elite of western North Carolina.

Descended from French Huguenots on his father's side and Irishmen on his mother's, William Lenoir was born in Brunswick, Virginia, in 1751, the youngest of ten children. Eight years later, his family moved to Edgecombe County in eastern North Carolina. When his father died in 1765, William took over operation of the family farm. He was facing a very uncertain future until 1771, when he married Anne Ballard, the daughter of a wealthy planter in neighboring Halifax County. Anne encouraged William to parlay his self-taught skills in mathematics into a surveying career, and she brought financial resources he could draw on. In 1773 he purchased his first slave, a forty-two-year-old woman who served as a nurse for his infant daughter Mary, and in 1775 his wife inherited a young slave woman (and all future children born to her). The two slaves accompanied the Lenoirs when they moved west in 1775 to the upper Yadkin River valley, a sparsely settled frontier region in the foothills of the Blue Ridge Mountains.

The Lenoirs had barely settled into their new community at Fisher Creek when the Revolutionary War broke out. William was an enthusiastic patriot who commanded militia troops in campaigns against the Cherokees, British loyalists, and the invading British army in 1780. His most celebrated military service came in the patriot victory at King's Mountain in October 1780, which ended Tory raids in the Carolina backcountry. His military record earned him the rank of general, along with the trust and respect that opened up political opportunities back home. He served as justice of the peace beginning in 1776 and was appointed county clerk. This latter position gave him access to information about how to register land claims, and with an insider's knowledge he soon began to buy land in large parcels. By 1780 he had amassed over 10,000 acres, most bought on credit with loans taken out of his father-in-law's estate.

Lenoir's military reputation and his expanding landholdings were the foundation for his rising political prominence. He served in both houses of the North Carolina General Assembly in the 1780s, was a delegate to the state's ratifying convention for the U.S. Constitution, and in 1791 was chosen as the first president of the board of trustees for the newly established University of North Carolina. Most of his time and energy, however, flowed into his activities as a planter-entrepreneur. As the soil on his original Wilkes County plantation began to wear out, he purchased a 200-acre tract of rich bottomland on the south side of the Yadkin and at the site of old Fort Defiance. Not content with selling corn and tobacco, he also operated a gristmill, sawmill, distillery, and leather shop to increase his profits. As one of the wealthiest men in the county, he lent money to many of his neighbors. His land-holdings, not only in Wilkes County but to the west across the Blue Ridge Mountains, made him one of the largest landlords in western North Carolina.

Smartly dressed for this 1840 photo, Tom Lenoir faced the world with a boyish openness that left him in a quandary as to the adult role he wanted to assume. (SOURCE: *North Carolina Collection, Wilson Library, University of North Carolina–Chapel Hill.*)

There's no doubting Walter's seriousness and intensity of purpose in this photo taken at the time of his graduation from the University of North Carolina. (SOURCE: *North Carolina Collection, Wilson Library, University of North Carolina–Chapel Hill.*)

While waiting for land values to rise, he rented his more accessible land to tenants on short-term leases. Cash was scarce, and he accepted corn as rent. To enhance the investment potential of the land, he insisted that his tenants plant and then plow under a soil-enriching crop such as rye, enclose cleared fields with fences, and preserve timber and other natural resources. He revealed the same patience and foresight as he accumulated slaves. Lenoir preferred to purchase young slaves or accept them as payment for debts. Their value was likely to rise and they could be trained in whatever skills were needed on the plantation. By 1790 he owned twelve slaves, half of whom were under the age of twelve.

Lenoir's political career peaked when he was elected speaker of the North Carolina Senate in 1790. He lost his Senate seat five years later and never again held elective office. Accustomed to holding political office as his just due for faithful community service, Lenoir was incapable of adjusting to the aggressive campaigning methods of selling himself to voters that arose out of two-party political competition in the 1790s. Still, he retained wide respect as the founding patriarch of the Lenoir family. His children married into some of the wealthiest families of western North Carolina and solidified the Lenoirs' power through an interlocking kin network of political and business connections. Two sons, William Ballard and Thomas, married daughters of Waightstill Avery, the largest slaveholder in neighboring Burke County. His daughters Ann and Sarah linked the family's fortunes with those of the Joneses, who had large holdings of land and slaves in Wilkes County as well as South Carolina. Another daughter, Martha, married Israel Pickens, a North Carolina member of Congress who moved his young bride to a plantation in Alabama after the War of 1812.

William's three sons found it difficult to break free from their father's influence and power in a pattern typical in the planting regions of the antebellum South. Land was the key to security and wealth and there were few other opportunities to acquire status and honor; consequently sons had to wait patiently for their share of the paternal estate. The eldest, William Ballard, accompanied his father on surveying trips to western North Carolina, settled into his father's former post as clerk of the court, and managed a neighboring plantation for his father. He was thirty-five before he asserted his independence, moving his family to the mouth of the Holston River in eastern Tennessee to establish a 5,000-acre estate on land deeded to him by his father. Perhaps he was motivated to break free by the example of Thomas, his younger brother. When Thomas married in 1806, his father-in-law gave the young couple land on the Pigeon River in western North Carolina. Accompanied by slaves and livestock, Thomas moved west the next year with high hopes of becoming a successful mountain planter.

Walter Raleigh, the youngest son, spent most of his adult years in Wilkes County. Prodded by his father, he tried clerking for a merchant in Morganton, but the tedious work left him bored and restless. Besides, as he admitted, he couldn't tell a "B from a bull's foot." After marrying a physician's daughter in 1815, he pleased his father immensely by settling down to the life of a Wilkes County farmer when he took over the plantation formerly managed by his brother William Ballard. But a growing family and a declining income (as the soil of the plantation became depleted) left him anxious to explore better prospects. In 1834, at the age of forty-eight, he moved with his wife, eight children, and twenty-three slaves to Boone County, Missouri.

By the time Walter Raleigh departed, Thomas had been back at Fort Defiance under his father's watchful eye for more than a decade. The move to what Thomas called those "cold mountains" had not gone well. The income from his tenant rentals and sales of grain and livestock failed to keep up with his expenses. Afflicted by poor health and rising debt, he considered a move to Tennessee to be close to his brother William Ballard. But his father, who never found an overseer he could trust to manage his plantation, convinced his reluctant son in 1822 to return home and relieve him of day-to-day operation of the plantation. In addition to appealing to his son's loyalty, he offered Thomas a partnership that would deed to him 960 acres of land, including the home plantation, and grant him a quarter interest in the livestock and crops. With a wife and six children to support, Thomas found the offer too attractive to turn down. That he had surrendered his independence for security was driven home when his father built an addition to the west end of Fort Defiance as living quarters for himself, his wife, and their unmarried daughter Mary.

Thomas's children, like those of General Lenoir, strategically married into other elite families. His eldest daughter, Selina Louisa, married a planter from the Alabama black belt, a plantation district named after the blackness of its fertile prairie soils. Mary Ann tied the family to another of the leading slaveholders in Wilkes County through her marriage to James Gwyn. Only Laura's marriage to Joe Norwood, a struggling storekeeper in the central Piedmont town of Hillsborough, failed to add to the family's status and influence. Sarah, his youngest daughter, stayed home and cared for her parents as they aged.

All of Thomas's sons had to struggle to establish their own identities. His eldest, William Avery (born in 1808), confided to his father in his early twenties that he was experiencing "a peculiar state of mind, which is still unaccountable to me. Whether it was a temporary imbecility, or partial derangement of my mind, or a delusion of my own imagination, I am not fully able to determine."

As he poured out his thoughts to his father, he recognized on some level that his unsettled mental condition was related to his fear of failure. He felt "unqualified in a great measure to do any kind of business which would be profitable; and you say that you don't think that I'll do for a farmer; and above all, you know that I have my natural indolence to deal with." By a few months later, the feeling seemed to have passed as he began "to feel like I can be of some account if I exert myself."

Over the years William's moods would swing from unbounded optimism to deep depression, from elation to despair. When he felt confident that he could carve out his own success and be of service to others, he plunged into schemes involving land, slaves, and moneylending. In the 1830s recently opened plantation districts of Alabama and Mississippi saw surging cotton prices that touched off a speculative frenzy to buy land and slaves. William, swept up in the euphoria, traveled to Alabama in early 1837 and boarded at the home of his cousins in the black belt town of Greensboro. He quickly sold not only the wagon and horses he had brought but also the slaves, whom his father had expected him to hire out. Upon hearing this, his parents cautioned him not to neglect the ethical standards of a slaveholding gentleman. "I hope," his mother wrote, "my dear William has not departed from those strict principles of Justice, which has hitherto regulated all his important transactions, by becoming for a time an *Alabamian or any other ian*, and therefore conclude that either your man Harry was willing to be sold, or that he had displeased you." In the moral universe of the Lenoirs, only dire financial necessity justified the sale of obedient slaves without their consent.

With the proceeds of his sales added to the money his father had given him to invest, William had over $10,000. On January 1, 1838, he loaned most of it out in notes payable to planters and would-be planters. Secured by the endorsement of family members or friends and registered with the clerk of the county court, such loans were common in the rural South where currency, whether specie or banknotes, was always scarce. Promissory notes between individuals met the demand for credit and functioned as a substitute for money.

William felt his investments were a sure thing, including money loaned to Andrew Calhoun, the son of former Vice President John C. Calhoun of South Carolina. "My debtors are all considered perfectly good," he wrote his father, "and if so I have made more this year than I could make in N.C. in three." But even as he wrote, the speculative binge of the mid-1830s was beginning to unravel. Before the year was out, cotton prices crashed, dragging down with them land and slave prices and the financial ability of debtors to meet their obligations. William learned the bitter lesson that a family name was no guarantee of repayment. For years he was unable to collect a cent from Andrew Calhoun. "I certainly have had more difficulty & embarrassment in my intercourse with him than any other man I ever dealt with," William fumed, "and why! because he is the humour'd spoilt child of a great man."

The financial crash of 1837 ushered in a decade of hard times and tight money across the South and most of the nation. Six years passed before William collected much from his Alabama debtors. In the meantime, his own debts mounted as, always anticipating that the bottom had been reached, he made large purchases of land. By the spring of 1842, his situation looked hopeless. With "a mind born down and oppressed by sorrows and shattered by nervous excitement," he felt that he was at the breaking point as he described a "black despair" that terrified him. "I feel most of the time like I had not a nerve in me—mind and energy seem at such times to desert me entirely and I spend day after day in a sort of horrid stupor which renders life a burden and from which I am aroused by some horrid vision." He could not bear being alone, but when he ventured out into company he experienced a mortification that was "worse than death." Further disgrace awaited him if he became a burden to his parents instead of a source of comfort and support. Little wonder that he had toyed with the idea of suicide, as he confessed to his parents.

Even in his darkest moments, William rejected the easy way out: his father's standing offer for him to return home and work at Fort Defiance. What he feared even more than the pressure of his creditors was the threat of being treated like a child by his father. In a phrase that reeked, however unconsciously, of the demeaning language whites used with adult slaves, his mother had written her thirty-one-year-old son, "Father says I must tell you *to be a good Boy and not to go for to think you are a man, and go out and get married.*" William shot back that he was "quite *old enough*" to make up his own mind regarding a wife, and he pointedly added that he considered his situation near Greensboro, Alabama, as "my adopted home."

Then William turned the tables by reminding his father that he, Thomas, had allowed himself to be ruled and controlled by the whims of his father. When General Lenoir had coaxed his son back to Fort Defiance, Thomas agreed to manage both his father's slaves and his own, a total of about fifty. That was far too many to be employed profitably in agricultural operations at the plantation. The general had indicated he would soon dispose of most of his slaves but never did. It was his grandson William Avery, not Thomas, who confronted the old man over the issue. His father had been saddled with "a great cross," he complained. Keeping all the slaves at work required cultivating almost all the land at Fort Defiance. Labor-saving and soil-conserving measures such as cultivating only the best land, putting in more small grains and fodder crops, devoting more fields to pasture, and increasing the stock of hogs by feeding less corn to slaves were all precluded as long as Thomas felt responsible for the general's slaves. The general was also imposing a burden on Thomas's wife and daughters, for it was they who, in addition to washing for and cleaning up after the stream of visitors to Fort Defiance, had to spin and cut out clothes for the slaves and nurse their sick. Poor mother, complained William, was making "too much a slave of herself."

The general was unmoved. If Thomas thought there were too many slaves at Fort Defiance, he replied, he could sell his own slaves. But Thomas refused. Like his father, he had convinced himself that he was a paternalistic master genuinely concerned about his slaves' well-being, a master who could provide better for his slaves than any new owner could or even the slaves themselves could if freed. When the general died in 1839, Thomas retained most of his father's slaves and supplemented his stagnant agricultural income from Fort Defiance by hiring out slaves and lending money. To William, this simply confirmed that Thomas was out of touch with economic reality and in no position to tell him what to do with his life.

William's crisis of 1842 passed. Loans from his father and family connections tided him over until he recouped some of his Alabama losses in 1843. Once again, he entered into a cycle of feverish activity followed by crippling depression. He scouted out land for investment in the mountains of his native state and to the west in Missouri, Illinois, and Iowa. Back in North Carolina, he threw himself into promoting internal improvements, soliciting contracts to locate and grade roads, and buying up land and old farms near Fort Defiance. In his buoyant dreams he was a model landlord who improved the lives of his tenant families, "say fifty or more souls whose moral destiny at least it will be in my power in some degree to control—can aid them in the establishment of a good school for the improvement of their minds; give employment to children that would otherwise be idle—and encourage them to habits of industry." After several months, reality set in: overblown hopes, bad investments, mounting debts, and the need to be bailed out by his father and friends. Any chance he might have had of breaking out of the cycle ended when his young wife, Jane Derr, died in 1850 from tuberculosis, after two years of a childless marriage. Her early death left him with "a loneliness that I will not attempt to describe."

Thomas Isaac, the second eldest son, was born in 1817. Like William, he chafed under the demands of a strong-willed father. Restless and unsettled through his late twenties, he had temporary bouts of the blues, but he never became as despondent as William. His father introduced him to managerial responsibilities as a teenager by sending him out to the Haywood plantation on the East Fork of the Pigeon River with instructions on how to care for the livestock and conduct business affairs with old neighbors and tenants. Urged by his older brother to improve his prospects by furthering his education, Tom enrolled at the Bingham School in Hillsborough in 1837 and spent the next year attending the University of North Carolina in Chapel Hill. In the closest he ever came to making a career decision, he expressed an interest in becoming an engineer by attending the U.S. Military Academy at West Point, the leading school for an engineering education in antebellum America. Citing expenses—$500 a year exclusive of clothing—and doubting whether Tom would ever succeed in such a competitive field, his father expressed grave reservations, and Tom refused to press the point. As a result, he simply drifted through much of the 1840s.

Tom tried his hand at clerking in Asheville and Wilkesboro, helped out his father at Fort Defiance and the East Fork, and traveled with William to Alabama several times. The state's black belt soils were mighty tempting to a planter's son accustomed to the worn-out lands of Wilkes County. As Tom put it on one of his trips, "the common soil of some farms here would be valuable manure in N.C." He almost bought land but worried about falling ill in Alabama's hot, humid climate. The same fear of coming down with yellow fever or malaria prevented him from volunteering for the Mexican War in 1846. Grudgingly, he agreed in 1849 to move out to the East Fork of the Pigeon River and manage his father's holdings there.

As his father's agent, Tom was responsible for managing and renting out 5,000 acres of land, buying and selling livestock, supervising the labor of about a dozen slaves, and collecting rents and debts from tenant families. It was a demanding job, and initially Tom yearned to be "more permanently" somewhere else, as he told

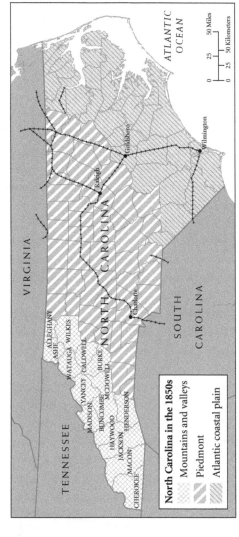

North Carolina in the 1850s.
Prior to the Civil War, western North Carolina remained isolated from the rest of the state.

his father in 1851, with "a prospect of doing more good for myself or some body else than I have here." But lacking the confidence to strike out on his own, he settled into his role as dutiful son.

Tom had a good eye for evaluating livestock, especially horses. He was happiest on the East Fork when he was selecting and breeding the sheep, hogs, cattle, mules, and horses that provided the plantation with meat, wool, leather, and, when sold in outside markets, trading profits. Managing the slaves and tenants was more troublesome. He, like slave owners across the South, found that slaves tested their masters' patience. Through feigned illnesses and studied ignorance they habitually tried to lighten their workload. The Lenoir slaves in Haywood had taken advantage of the lax controls of Augustus Hargrove, the overseer Thomas employed on his absentee plantation in the mid-1840s. This became clear to Tom when he sent two hands to break up ground for a new field. Upon checking their progress, he "ripped & snorted" when he saw them haphazardly running a plow over large piles of manure on the site, piles so high that the tip of the plow could not even reach the ground. Their explanation was that for the past five years Hargrove had told them not to bother to spread the manure because it would be scattered sufficiently by the plow.

As he tightened up work habits and undertook badly needed repairs on the plantation, Tom found most of the slaves to be compliant workers. He knew, however, that compliancy ultimately rested on their fear of physical punishment and he needed to make an example of slaves who pushed their master too far. "One trouble," as Tom called it, concerned the slave Erwin. His unnamed offense so enraged Tom that he forced himself to cool down for a few days before he gave Erwin a "sound thrashing" after tying him to the horse rack in the stables. Reflecting his need to see himself as a caring but stern master who had the best interests of his slave at heart, Tom described the whipping as if it were therapeutic for both himself and the slave. Erwin, Tom convinced himself, was truly contrite and afterward "said he was glad it was over, & that he felt better *satisfied* than he had done since [his defiance] on that Tuesday morning." As for Tom, he congratulated himself on the cool, dispassionate way he had administered a terrible chastisement.

Tom won his test of wills with Erwin, but Isaac, "a first rate ditcher, a pretty good hewer, & has worked some at the carpenter's trade," frightened him. He was "a little spoiled" and had to be sold off "for the good of the others" before he infected all the slaves with his rebellious attitude. Intimidated by Isaac's strength and swagger, Tom doubted that he'd physically be able to whip him and instead hired two men who apparently specialized in the task of bringing dangerous slaves to heel. Under the guise of visitors, they arrived one evening at the Den, Tom's farmhouse, for dinner. The next morning, as unsuspecting Isaac ate breakfast, Tom pointed him out as "the boy that must be whipped." He sprang up and bolted for the door, but the men Tom had hired disarmed Isaac of a knife, wrestled him to the ground, stripped, and whipped him. They then carted him off to the jail in Asheville and, within a week, he was bought for $1,100 by a local planter who intended to sell him for a profit in Alabama. Pleased, Tom had every reason to believe that "the effect will be good on the other slaves."

Tom's tenants, some ten families, required a lighter touch. Most had been renting land for a number of years, often because they owed money to Tom's father but were unable to pay it back. Following his father's advice, Tom did not press them for repayment in cash. In addition to proving fruitless, such pressure would also besmirch the name of the Lenoirs as benevolent patriarchs. Instead, Tom managed their debts by accepting livestock as payment and by hiring them as day laborers on the plantation to work off some of their debts. He also tried to improve their work habits, counseling them on the virtues of sobriety and the evils of chewing tobacco. Out of a sense of duty to the rising generation, he established a Sunday school library up at Old Man Anderson's tenant farm and taught a Sunday school class there. The tenants, most of whom were Methodists, also gathered at Anderson's to hear the circuit rider preach. In addition to moral guidance, Tom distributed surplus corn whenever his tenants came up short. As his father explained, the tenants expected such assistance as their customary right, and if he failed to supply them with corn, they'd move on and find a landlord who would.

For all the attention Tom devoted to his tenants, he could never overcome the resentment attached to the Lenoirs' great wealth. Tenants and local farmers continually harassed him with disputes over land and the validity of his father's land titles and survey lines. Many agreed with old Josiah Anderson, who openly complained that "it's a *serious & candid fact* that Tom Lenoir has imposed on the people of the E. Fork by preventing their getting lands on which they could make a support." No wonder the tenants expected a yearly ration of corn. Anderson might have been cantankerous, but the Lenoirs did not fear him. David Reese was a different story. Warned by his father that Reese was "malicious and lazy" and not above killing and maiming a man's stock out of spite, Tom treaded lightly with the entire Reese family. They were part of a large clan that would be "dangerous enemies" if any were offended. Tom's father had kept them on as tenants in the 1840s out of a perverse combination of pity and fear. In a shrewd piece of negotiation, Tom soon released them as tenants by overpaying them for the improvements they had put up on their rented land.

As Tom reconciled himself to settling down on the East Fork, his younger brothers, Walter and Rufus, were already fixed in their family roles. They were part of the last cohort of the Lenoir children, born at Fort Defiance along with their older sister Sarah. Companions and playmates in childhood, the three of them forged the closest sibling bonds within the family.

Walter was the favored child. Sarah abided by an unspoken agreement to remain home and look after her parents, who were in their fifties by the time she was in her teens. Rufus, the baby of the family, was a slow learner, fond of riding horses and making mischief. Walter, serious, bookish, and frail, was the son singled out by his father to adorn the family with the accomplishments of a famed scholar. Thomas had deemed tutoring at home a sufficient education for his oldest boys, William and Tom, whom he expected to take over his plantation affairs.

Walter, on the other hand, left home to board with his sister Laura Norwood in Hillsborough while he received a rigorous education in the Classics at Bingham School, a private academy. Almost painfully aware that he alone of the children was to have the advantage of a formal education, he prodded his father into sending Rufus to the Bingham School as well. When Rufus began his classes in 1838, Laura reported that Walter "seems equally as much interested in Rufus' improvement as his own, and it would give you pleasure to see with what unhurried patience he assists, explains & encourages him in his studies." With Walter's help, Rufus did well, but he never was as interested in book learning. After dropping in and out of the Bingham School for the next five years, he spent one term at the University of North Carolina in Chapel Hill, before returning to Fort Defiance in 1845 to take up the only life he ever felt qualified for, that of a country farmer. He was twenty when he began taking over the operation of the home plantation from his father.

Walter struggled to fulfill his father's expectations when he enrolled at the university at Chapel Hill in August 1839. Simply being there placed him in an elite group. His fellow students were also planters' sons who had been sent to college to acquire the Classical education of a true gentleman that would infuse in them values of personal honor and public virtue and train them in the skills of rhetoric and oratory they would draw upon in their future roles as public leaders. Such was the ideal. As Walter discovered to his dismay, however, the all-male student body, free from parental controls, frequently left off studying to carouse, drink, and defy any rules and regulations they found petty and infantilizing. Raised as a strict Episcopalian, he found it disgraceful that students played cards on Sunday evening while chapel was under way or stole horses from those attending a revival and rode them wildly down the streets of Chapel Hill. When three students were expelled in October 1842 for drunkenness and ringing the university bell, he wrote his father, rather priggishly, "Such is the state of morality in the only institution which our state has provided for the nurture of her future judges and lawgivers."

Well into his junior year Walter doubted if he wanted to finish his studies at the university. Part of the problem was his fellow students, "the young, the gay, and the idle," as he dubbed them. He was bored with attending recitations "chiefly passed in listening to the abominable blunders of those who know nothing of their studies," and convinced that he was coasting on what he had learned at the Bingham School. His courses offered him neither the mastery of sound business habits nor the moral lessons needed to strengthen his character.

But the problem ran deeper. Walter immensely enjoyed many of his readings and was attracted to the life of a cloistered scholar. While acknowledging that "this is the happiest part of my life," to remain at Chapel Hill "for mere enjoyment," he told his father, "would have been the height of injustice to you and to myself." The injustice in his mind consisted in following a personal whim that would deprive him of the sense of repaying his parents for having been "a burden and expense to you without rendering any thing in return." He alone among his brothers had not put in long hours helping on the plantation. Better to face up to his family responsibilities, he argued, and leave college for the study of law, a profession that would enable him "to be useful" to his parents.

But with his father's encouragement, the president of the university, David Swain, persuaded Walter to stay the course. He graduated in May 1843, delivering the valedictory address. His greatest gratification from his college honors was "the consciousness that it will be a source of pleasure to my parents." Although proud of his accomplishments, he criticized himself for squandering many advantages while in college. He pledged to his mother that "no four years of my life shall ever pass again, without being better improved."

Before setting out to improve his work habits, Walter went on a five-month tour of the Northern states with his brother Tom. Swinging up through the Shenandoah Valley of Virginia, they walked during the day and camped out at night. Once they reached Washington, they traveled by rail to Baltimore and points north to Boston. From Boston they headed west to Albany, New York, followed the Erie Canal to Buffalo for a visit to Niagara Falls, and then turned south and returned home through Kentucky and Tennessee. Whereas the trip reaffirmed for Thomas the virtues of a quiet rural life in North Carolina, Walter was struck by the signs of progress and improvement in the cities and countryside of the North, especially in New York, "without a rival … the first state in the union."

In the spring of 1844 Walter rejoined his sister Laura's family in Hillsborough, where he read law in preparation for taking the law exam before the justices of the state supreme court in Raleigh. He took a break from his studies in April to hear the Whig presidential candidate Henry Clay speak in Raleigh. Like the other Lenoirs, Walter was a committed Whig. Both his father and grandfather had railed against the Democrats as a party of unprincipled despots who catered to the "rabble" under the blustering, dangerous leadership of the arch-tyrant, Andrew Jackson. They denounced Jackson for defying national law in his destruction of the Second Bank of the United States, filling government offices with party hacks, and pursuing reckless financial policies that plunged the nation into a depression in 1837.

THE MAKING OF A CONFEDERATE

For the Lenoirs, only the Whigs could promise a responsible government that placed the well-being of the nation above sectional interests and parochial party concerns. Clay supported a protective tariff that benefited primarily the manufacturing states of the North, but in return he proposed distributing tariff revenues to the states in a fund for internal improvements. That was an appealing program in western North Carolina, where community leaders had long cited the need for better transportation as the key to economic progress. In November Walter voted for Clay out of "patriotism and a sense of duty."

Early on in his studies Walter decided that he was not cut out to be a lawyer. He found the details of the law to be stultifying and concluded that a lawyer had to inure himself "to find his premises among the details and rubbish that have been accumulating around the law for ages, to cram the storehouse of his memory with the commodities and old wares of every period since the feudal age." As at Chapel Hill, he almost backed out of his commitment but ultimately deferred to the advice of his father and friends. By 1846 he was licensed to practice in the superior courts of North Carolina.

His father correctly predicted that ten years would elapse before Walter was able to support himself from his legal fees. Not until 1854 did Walter's legal earnings cover his expenses. The law was a competitive profession in the late antebellum South, especially in the sparsely populated mountains of North Carolina. Young lawyers routinely hung around courthouses hoping to drum up business by helping collect debts, settle land disputes, and resolve contested claims over the physical fitness of a slave between buyer and seller. At first Walter fretted that he was trapped in a profession that "would be like a journey upon a treadmill, ending, where it set out." In 1852, when he was only twenty-nine, he characterized himself as an "old bachelor." He had just discovered his first gray hair and ruefully noted a cracked upper tooth that would soon share the fate of four lower ones he already had lost. In his worst moments of despondency he compared his life to "a weary, painful dream" in which he was guilty of shutting his heart "against the exercise of its natural affections, and freezing it into sterility." What depressed him was the fear that he would never earn enough to support a wife. And without the love of a woman, he felt his life would have little joy. "When, in reverie, I have pictured ideal happiness," he confided in his journal, "it never entered my thoughts to separate it from woman's love."

While establishing himself as a lawyer, Walter teamed up with his brothers to implement the changes William had long advocated in their father's management of the slaves at Fort Defiance. The problem, noted William in early 1850, was the need "to thin out the sable population of the Fort for many reasons of morality & expediency." It was time to "do something for the relief of the [white] women folks and get the means of doing something for yourselves—what say you? I think father would have no objections if his sons would do it." This was the same argument William had made to no avail in 1835. But now, with the intimidating presence of General Lenoir removed from the scene, William guessed that his father would agree to his plan.

But how to manage or dispose of the some fifty slaves at Fort Defiance? Nearly all of them were related to each other, and it was difficult to increase their numbers by finding husbands or wives for the small number of young, unattached slaves. Thomas refused to sell slaves who seemed loyal and faithful. In the meantime, his slaves as plantation workers were an unprofitable investment, "for if you set a reasonable price on them, and compare the interest on that sum with the net proceeds of their services (while they are not growing nor increasing) you will arrive at the conclusion that they are a bad stock in trade." He was open to any advice his sons had.

Walter was eager to act. In March 1850 his uncle, William B. Lenoir, jointly conveyed land in Ashe and Watauga counties to Walter and his son Israel. Walter soon bought out Israel's interest, paying for it in a note of $450, half of which was due in two years. He hoped to attract tenants to the land and convert it into a stock farm. With the long economic slump of the 1840s at an end, slaves were selling at attractive prices. He and William sold eleven slaves in the summer of 1850, those deemed the greatest threat to slave discipline at Fort Defiance. Walter paid off his note to cousin Israel and joined William in the fall on a land-buying trip to Ashe and Watauga.

With land to his name and his legal income increasing, Walter felt independent enough to consider marriage. On January 17, 1856, he proposed to Cornelia Christian, a Virginia cousin he had met on one of her frequent visits to relatives in North Carolina. After five years of courtship in which she repeatedly attempted to cheer up her often disconsolate suitor, Nealy, as he called her, must have been as relieved as Walter when he finally summoned up the courage to propose. The couple married on June 10, 1856, and Walter could not have been happier. "My cup of earthly bliss is now full and overflowing," he wrote in his journal. His only concern now was that his joy might cause him to be derelict in his religious duties of preparing his soul for heaven.

Following the birth of their daughter, Anna Tate, in November 1857, Walter and Nealy moved to Lenoir, down the road from Fort Defiance, where Walter had his law office. Living with Walter and Nealy in Lenoir was Cyrus, a young male slave. This was the first time Walter had actually managed a slave; previously, he had dealt with slaves only as an abstraction, a faceless source of capital that gave him the means of buying land and realizing his ambition of being a progressive landlord. In March 1858, Cyrus was caught breaking into the Harper store in Lenoir. On one hand, Walter reacted as slave owners often did when their authority was defied: he sold Cyrus. On the other hand, and undoubtedly encouraged to do so by Nealy, he faced up to his moral misgivings over slavery, which he had ignored as long as somebody else had to deal with the messy and morally numbing business of disciplining slaves and inflicting physical pain. When confronted with these inescapable realities, he and Nealy both decided they wanted none of it. Soon after selling Cyrus, Walter wrote his brother Tom that "I feel determined at present never to own another slave. Both Nealy and I have concluded after our limited experience with slaves, that the evil of being a master and mistress of slaves is greater than we are willing to bear unless imposed on us by some sterner necessity belonging to our lot than we know of. Our present feeling is that we will eventually make our home in a free state."

Any decision on moving to the North, however, had to be postponed because of health concerns. Their infant daughter fell gravely ill in the spring of 1858, and a brain disease claimed her life in May. At the same time Nealy's persistent cough was worsening. She had tuberculosis, and the usual therapy of immersion in the mineral waters of health spas in the Virginia mountains failed to arrest the disease. Desperately hoping that a warmer climate would help, Walter resolved to take Nealy to Cuba. They made it as far as Charleston, South Carolina, where she died in February 1859. At her wish, she was buried next to Anna in the Lenoir family cemetery at Fort Defiance.

Walter was nearly paralyzed with grief. He had lost "her whose life gave me a home, and my life an aim." Walter remembered her as an idealized saint who had selflessly willed her death so that her daughter would not be without a mother in heaven. Two months after her death, he put words to his "wretchedness" in a letter to Bolivar Christian, Nealy's brother. He had been rightfully punished, he believed, for his "ingratitude to the Giver in not making a full surrender of my heart to him." Despite the pleadings of his mother and sisters, Walter had refused to proclaim himself a Christian by allowing himself to be baptized and confirmed in his family's Episcopal church. Consequently Walter marveled that God had ever blessed him by bringing Nealy into his life. In the closest he came to an expression of self-consolation, he suggested to Bolivar that God had allowed him to know unbounded happiness with Nealy so that he might learn the "loveliness of virtue."

In working through his grief, Walter was visibly depressed. His friends worried about his "crippled condition" as he listlessly attended to his law practice. A sense of purpose returned to his life only when he prepared in the fall of 1860 for a trip to the North in search of a new home and a fresh start. He followed the rail lines west through Nashville and Louisville and then north to Indianapolis, Chicago, Milwaukee, and St. Paul, the rapidly growing cities of the Midwest. He returned down the Mississippi through Memphis and St. Louis. He found what he was looking for in St. Anthony, a small town ten miles up the Mississippi from St. Paul.

Although generally impressed with the fertility of Midwestern farms, he was disturbed by the many foreigners he encountered in rural areas. They were thrifty, industrious farmers with an uncanny knack of locating and holding onto much of the best land, but they struck Walter as clannish and unwilling to support internal improvements and public schools, clear evidence to him that they opposed progressive change for the public good. Most disturbing was what he decried as their "fanatical" views on the slavery question. He was still enough of a Southerner to equate any antislavery stand with abolitionism. In fact, the mostly German immigrant farmers in the Midwest were moderate on the slavery question. The cities, especially Chicago, impressed him with their visible signs of wealth and projects of public improvement, but land prices in the most attractive neighborhoods were too high and the businessmen too much driven by a love of profit and showy display for his taste.

What drew him to the upper Mississippi valley was its reputation for a climate free of the outbreaks of fever that swept through the bottomlands of the Midwest. It was here, as well in the area around St. Anthony, where Walter felt most comfortable with the town-country mix of enterprising settlers committed to growth and community improvement. The cold winters and springs would take some getting used to, but the more he mulled it over, the more convinced he became that he had found his future home. He planned on returning to Minnesota in the spring of 1861 to purchase property.

On both legs of his trip Walter was caught up in the political excitement of Stephen A. Douglas's presidential campaign.

He watched in amazement as torchlit processions packed with 25,000 Douglas supporters filled the streets of Midwestern cities. He was impressed with more than just the sheer energy of the Illinois senator's campaign. Although he had always been a Whig in his politics, Walter identified with much of the Northern Democrat's platform. Like Douglas, he favored promoting economic development. Like Douglas, he agreed that party extremists in both sections threatened the existence of the Union and that the best solution for the divisive issue of slavery's expansion was to allow the settlers in the territories to decide the issue for themselves. He returned to North Carolina in early November just in time to cast his vote for Douglas.

Walter reentered a slave society that was in the early stages of the crisis that would dissolve the Union by the spring of 1861. As anticipated, the North's antislavery candidate, the Republican Abraham Lincoln, won the presidential election. His victory worsened the financial contraction sparked by fears of an impending political crisis: much of the normal sectional trade dried up and made credit hard to get. Adding to the gloom was a poor harvest—for the third year in a row—in North Carolina. A long summer drought across most of the South had made this the worst of the three.

Rufus reported in early October that "corn is scarce & money is said to be scarcer." He, along with other planters, sold off their mules and hogs, the "corn-eaters," to conserve their reserves and tried vainly to call in loans from their debtors. Rufus had reason to worry about the rural poor in his neighborhood. Close to half of the farmers nearby owned no land. With little or no cash to buy corn or wheat at a merchant's drought-inflated prices, and with no land to raise their own food, they depended on the planters for assistance when crops were short. Distributing corn and wheat to the poor farmers and renters working the flinty soils up on the hilly ridges was a time-honored tradition for the Lenoirs. "Only five of the *common sort*" arrived at the fort today, William wrote, describing a typical episode. "One wanted lard; another a bushel of corn; another a half bushel of Irish 'taters'; another about a peck of sweet-*taters* 'if you please mam'; and the other hadn't reported when I left; of course you know, they all went away satisfied; *until they come again*. Bless the '*old Fort!*' (some will say perhaps) for they remember the Scripture, '*The poor ye have always with you*'!'" But the hard times in 1860 only worsened the political crisis.

Because his trip had filled him with optimism, Walter at first held out some hope for the Union in the wake of Lincoln's election. Not brother William: he lapsed into a bad case of the blues. Rufus, who stood to inherit the home plantation after the death of his aging father, was now a husband with two small children. Having loaned out $9,000, he was also one of the largest moneylenders in the county. He had much to conserve and protect. His spirits, already low before the election, plunged when the results were in. He expected his future to crumble as he lived to see "all the glory for which our forefathers fought, bled, & died buried in eternal shame & ruin."

Walter's optimism lasted only two weeks. "The political troubles of the day," he believed, would force him to give up his plans to move to Minnesota. "If we are to have disunion, I will cast my fortunes with the South, at least till the question is settled, and peace restored, or till the question has settled me. I don't want to live in a country where I will have to get a pass from Abraham Lincoln, or the likes of him, before I can come to North Carolina."

As he sensed would be the case, the deepening political crisis forced Walter to confront a decision he dreaded to make. But there was no avoiding it—as he would discover in the spring of 1861.

NOTES

Although the major sources for this and subsequent chapters came out of the Lenoir Family Papers housed at the University of North Carolina at Chapel Hill, my primary source for the life and career of General Lenoir was Richard A. Shrader, "William Lenoir, 1751–1839" (Ph.D. diss., University of North Carolina, 1978). Additional material was found in Thomas Felix Henderson, *Happy Valley: History and Genealogy* (Durham, N.C.: Seeman, 1940).

The family's strategy of establishing extensive kinship networks with other leading slaveholders through marriage was common among Southern planters and can be traced for western North Carolina in John C. Inscoe, *Mountain Masters, Slavery, and the Sectional Crisis in Western North Carolina* (Knoxville: University of Tennessee Press, 1989), pp. 117–20. Inscoe is also superb on documenting the underappreciated role of planters in shaping the economy and politics of Southern Appalachia.

For the difficulty planters' sons experienced in establishing their own identities, see Bertram Wyatt-Brown, *Southern Honor: Ethics and Behavior in the Old South* (New York: Oxford University Press, 1982), especially chapter 7. Wyatt-Brown's linkage of themes of depression and melancholy with literary genius in *Hearts of Darkness: Wellsprings of a Southern Literary Tradition* (Baton Rouge: Louisiana State University Press, 2003) was also helpful for placing William Lenoir's bouts of crippling depression in a wider cultural context.

In their dealings with both black slaves and white tenants, the Lenoirs saw themselves as benevolent patriarchs. Eugene D. Genovese, *Roll, Jordan, Roll: The World the Slaves Made* (New York: Pantheon, 1974) stands as the classic account of the mutual dependency between masters and slaves that lay at the heart of Southern conceptions of paternalism. Willie Lee Rose's account of the historical evolution of paternalism in *Slavery and Freedom*, ed. William W. Freehling (New York: Oxford University Press, 1982) is still very useful. Although the masters held the upper hand, the slaves were not powerless. As Tom discovered when he took over his father's plantation in Haywood County, they were constantly pushing the patience of their owners. For all their protestations of benevolence, the Lenoirs, like slave owners across the South, had no compunctions against selling off recalcitrant slaves. Michael Tadman's pathbreaking *Speculators and Slaves: Masters, Traders, and Slaves in the Old South* (Madison: University of Wisconsin Press, 1989) documents the massive extent of the internal slave trade and its importance in maintaining the profitability of slavery in the Upper South. For the ambivalent place of slave trading in the moral universe of the South, see Robert H. Gudmestad, *A Troublesome Commerce: The Transformation of the Interstate Slave Trade* (Baton Rouge: Louisiana State University Press, 2004).

Although much less has been done on the relations between antebellum planters and their white tenants, Joseph D. Reid Jr. provides a finely grained analysis of fifty-seven of the tenant leases signed by Thomas and William Lenoir in Haywood County in "Antebellum Southern Rental Contracts," *Explorations in Economic History*, January 1976, pp. 69–83. Wilma A. Dunaway, *The First American Frontier: Transition to Capitalism in Southern Appalachia, 1700–1860* (Chapel Hill: University of North Carolina Press, 1996), leaves no doubt of the pervasive landlessness among agricultural families in the mountain regions of the South before the Civil War.

In their desire for diversified economic growth and their ambivalence over the permanence of slavery, the Lenoirs closely paralleled the attitudes of Southern Whiggery sketched out in John Ashworth, *Slavery, Capitalism, and Politics in the Antebellum Republic*, vol. 1, *Commerce and Compromise, 1820–1850* (New York: Cambridge University Press, 1995) and closely examined in Michael F. Holt, *The Rise and Fall of the American Whig Party: Jacksonian Politics and the Onset of the Civil War* (New York: Oxford University Press, 1999). The party's fortunes in North Carolina are covered in Marc W. Kruman, *Parties and Politics in North Carolina, 1836–1865* (Baton Rouge: Louisiana State University Press, 1983). Imagining a South in which capitalist development *gradually* displaced reliance on slave labor, Whigs desperately tried to find a middle ground between Northern abolitionism and Southern separatism. They ran out of options for compromise once Lincoln was elected, and Whigs in the Upper South, like Walter, were forced to choose a side as the secession crisis deepened.

· *Two* ·

CONFEDERATE SOLDIER

—⁓—

Cᴀʟʟs ғᴏʀ ɪᴍᴍᴇᴅɪᴀᴛᴇ sᴇᴄᴇssɪᴏɴ ᴀʀᴏᴜsᴇᴅ ʟɪᴛᴛʟᴇ ᴇɴᴛʜᴜsɪᴀsᴍ in North Carolina. Lincoln's election posed no immediate danger in a state where only 28 percent of the white families owned slaves. The planters most likely to be threatened by Republican moves against slavery were concentrated in the eastern coastal counties, not surprisingly the one region in the state where secession found much initial support. As they had during the sectional crisis of the 1850s, old Whig planting families like the Lenoirs counseled moderation and tried to stake out a middle ground between those they denounced as extremists in both sections—ambitious, hot-headed radicals in the Lower South and the meddling, fanatical abolitionists in the North.

Sallie Lenoir, Rufus's wife, had every reason to "dread the dark future," as she wrote upon hearing of Lincoln's election. "If the South would only keep cool and try him first, I think we need not fear so much," she said, "but I cannot hope that." Led by the fire-brands in South Carolina, the cotton states of the Lower South quickly dashed any hopes that the Union would remain intact before Lincoln's inauguration in early March. South Carolina's secession convention took the state out of the Union on December 20, 1860, and the rest of the Lower South scheduled elections on the secession issue for early January.

On December 22, as the Union was beginning to unravel, Walter played a leading role in what was billed as a Union meeting at the courthouse in Lenoir. Heading the list of the resolutions that he introduced was the assertion that only "a willful violation" of any of the provisions of the U.S. Constitution by a "sectional majority" could justify the secession of a state. He, along with most other Whigs and moderate Democrats, believed that such a violation had not yet occurred. Nonetheless, the slaveholding states believed they had grievances that had to be addressed if the Union were to be preserved in a sectional compromise. Lenoir's resolutions cited efforts by Northern states to block the enforcement of the Fugitive Slave Act of 1850 as just one example of how "the violent and continued agitation of the institution of slavery" had produced the present political crisis. His key resolution was a demand for a "final settlement" of all the sectional issues that arose out of the slavery issue.

The resolutions, which easily carried, were typical of those passed at public meetings in western and central North Carolina. The Unionism they expressed was genuine but conditioned on the willingness of the incoming Republican administration to offer a satisfactory sectional settlement and to stop short of using military force to "coerce" any seceded state back into the Union. For leadership, these Unionists turned to Representative Zebulon B. Vance, from Buncombe County in western North Carolina. Like his constituents, Vance believed that for a state to secede was to "invite anarchy and confusion, carnage, civil war and financial ruin with the breathless hurry of men fleeing from a pestilence."

When Congress assembled in early December, Vance hoped that some compromise could be worked out. He and Walter exchanged ideas on what would be acceptable to the Southern states, many of which were embodied in the Crittenden Compromise, a series of resolutions and proposed constitutional amendments meant to allay Southern fears over the safety of slavery in the Union. Its most critical feature called for extending the Missouri Compromise line through the national territories. The rejection of the compromise by both Republican members of Congress and those still in Congress from the Lower South ended the best chance for isolating South Carolina as the only state to secede. Informing Walter on December 26 of the plan's collapse, a dejected Vance reported that Republicans had no intention of offering terms. He now viewed the dissolution of the Union as a foregone conclusion.

As six more states seceded in January, all signs pointed to the rapid formation of a slaveholders' republic in the Cotton South. Walter agreed with Vance that the economic interests of cotton planters would shape and dictate the new confederation's policies. And those policies revolved around slavery. The low-country planters of South Carolina favored reopening the African slave trade to lower the prices of slaves, eliminating tariffs through free trade, and adding slave territory to cement the South's monopoly on the world cotton supply. If enacted, this program would have choked off efforts in the Upper South to channel the profits reaped from selling high-priced slaves to the Lower South into efforts to reorient its economy toward agricultural diversification and manufacturing. On economic grounds alone Walter felt that North Carolina and the other states of the Upper South should avoid a political alliance with the cotton states. In addition, he was "utterly opposed to reopening the [African] slave trade" and had "no desire to engage in the silly project of trying in vain to carry slavery into Mexico and Central America, two long inhabited countries, which have rejected slavery once, and won't receive it again, even if the North remain quiet."

Throughout the early months of 1861 Walter clung to the hope that the Union could be restored peacefully. Rather than give in to the "mad fanaticism" of extremists in either section, he favored the middle course first proposed by Maryland and Virginia Unionists in December. Their plan called for the formation of a central confederacy made up of the border states in the North and South, casting off the fanatics in New England and the Deep South deemed responsible for the current crisis. What would be left would be a set of homogeneous interests that had always placed the Union above sectional interests and rigid political dogmas. Out of such a plan, Walter wrote Vance in January, would emerge a "great central conservative party." Once this party had settled sectional differences among themselves, they would be in a position to broker a restoration of the Union. Here, he believed, was "the best foundation for the ultimate reconstruction of the Union in its present integrity of territory, when the madness of the hour has passed away."

Walter's optimism for a Union-saving compromise grew in February as the voters in the Upper South rejected secession in a series of state elections. Hoping in part to influence the elections, Republicans in Congress were now adopting a more conciliatory stance. Walter saw no reason why the delegates at the special meeting in Washington, D.C., initiated by Virginia and dubbed the Peace Conference, could not come up with a definitive sectional compromise modeled on the Crittenden proposals. After all, the seven cotton states that came together at Montgomery, Alabama, in February 1861 to form the Confederate States of America seemingly did not possess the economic strength to survive long as an independent nation. The eight slave states that remained in the Union contained two-thirds of the South's free white population, harvested most of its food crops, and produced nearly all of its manufactured goods. Most critically, any compromise that kept these states in the Union would deprive the Confederacy access to such vital commercial centers as St. Louis, Louisville, Memphis, and Nashville.

But would such a compromise provoke the secessionists into precipitating a war? The inland ports, reasoned Walter, were the "brilliant prizes" for which the secessionists would wage a war. "They know that war will defeat the compromise. They know that if they can inaugurate a state of War with the North that the border Slave States cannot stand on the side of the North in that war.... War then *must* separate us from the North."

Such a war was now Walter's greatest fear, for it would force North Carolina to leave the Union. Rather than allowing itself to be dragged into that war, Walter argued, the state should proclaim a policy of armed neutrality and align itself with the other border slave states. Once the secessionists accepted that the Upper South wanted nothing to do with the war, they would come to their senses and an eventual reunion would be possible.

Walter admitted to Vance that he had "only a faint hope" that North Carolina would remain neutral in a military showdown between the Federal government and the Confederacy. He was even less confident that Federal troops would be withdrawn from Southern forts, a policy demanded by Southern Unionists as the surest way of preventing a war. As states seceded from the Union, they laid claim to all Federal property within their boundaries, including arsenals and forts. With the exception of two isolated forts in the Florida Keys, only Fort Pickens off the coast of Pensacola, Florida, and Fort Sumter in Charleston harbor remained in Federal possession at the end of the Buchanan presidency. Of the two, Fort Sumter was the more politically charged. In the eyes of the secessionists, its retention by the Federal government was an unacceptable threat to the military security and political sovereignty of the Confederacy. Here, thought Walter, was the likely flashpoint for a sectional war.

In mid-March, Lincoln's secretary of state, William H. Seward, gave what seemed to be assurances that Fort Sumter was to be evacuated. In fact, Seward's attempt (behind Lincoln's back) to buy time to negotiate backfired disastrously in April, when Lincoln ordered a relief expedition to Fort Sumter. Unionists across the Upper South felt betrayed, and their anger turned to rage when Lincoln issued a proclamation on April 15, 1861, calling on the states for troops to suppress what he defined as a rebellion against Federal authority. It was this proclamation, more than the Confederate bombardment of Fort Sumter, which shattered Southern Unionism and drove four more slave states—Virginia, Arkansas, Tennessee, and North Carolina—to secede. Regardless of their political leanings, an overwhelming

majority of whites in the Upper South viewed Lincoln's proclamation as a declaration of war and a call for the invasion of
their homes, the abolition of slavery, and the end of the liberties
they held dear.

Walter was preparing to move to Haywood County and
become a mountain farmer when he heard of Lincoln's proclamation and "became certain that the war was actually upon us."
His reaction took the form of the religious conversion he had so
long yearned for. As he told Rufus, "For ten or fifteen minutes
I studied myself harder than I ever did in my life. I remember
that large drops of sweat stood on my forehead.... I reflected that,
under God, I owed my life, my care, my enjoyment, my property to the laws and institutions of my country; and I paid the
debt. I gave them all back to my country to be used, if needed, in
asserting its liberty, and its power to protect me and those that
were dear to me." He had made his decision. He would fight for
his country, the Confederacy that he had scorned before Lincoln's North was transformed in his mind into the invader of
his homeland.

Walter would have enlisted immediately, except for sobering
news from Fort Defiance. For years, brother William had wrestled
with his personal demons, manically buying land and making
loans in the hopes of striking it rich, only to become depressed
when his dreams foundered and his wife died. The doubt that he
would ever be happy returned in the midst of the secession crisis,
stronger than ever. For weeks, he had been suffering from a bad
case of the blues, but the other Lenoirs took no special notice.
They had seen him like this before, and his current depression
seemed no worse than his past bouts.

The death of their father in January hit William hard. For years he had been a beacon of stability, the patriarch of the family whom William instinctively leaned on. Over the years, as William's debts worsened, his father had always been there to bail him out. Now his father was gone, and with secession frenzy sweeping through the country and hard times staring everyone in the face, William feared that his shaky finances would crash down around him. How could he ever hope to collect his debts, especially now that the war had started? What would happen if the Yankees invaded? Others may have been fired up to fight for the preservation of slavery, states' rights, or an independent South, but not William. He wanted only to live a life in the tradition his father had, but luck had deserted him.

On the morning of May 1, William went to the home of Joe and Laura Norwood, his neighbors for the past decade after they had relocated from Hillsborough. He took Norwood's rifle and went out front under the walnut tree. No one spotting him with a rifle would have been alarmed, since he often found relief from his depression by going outside to shoot. As Walter recalled, this was his way of trying "to amuse himself." This time he put the rifle barrel to his temple and fired. His body was discovered in the afternoon.

William's death was shocking. In the absence of a suicide note, some of the Lenoirs tried to convince themselves that somehow it was all an accident. Beyond working through their grief, however, they had more mundane matters to deal with: debts to be sorted out, lands to be divided, and tenants to be managed. Walter spent much of the summer and fall in a fruitless attempt to settle William's debts by selling off land in the estate. It would take years to untangle William's landholdings.

William's body was discovered in the front yard of Oak Lawn, the Norwoods' home in Lenoir.
(SOURCE: *North Carolina Collection, Wilson Library, University of North Carolina–Chapel Hill.*)

With fewer responsibilities demanding his attention, Tom was free to enlist earlier than Walter. His decision to raise a volunteer company in Haywood surprised the other Lenoirs almost as much as his sudden marriage to sixteen-year-old Lizzie Garrett in January 1861. His sister Laura thought that Tom was foolish to think of going off to war at the age of forty-three; he could better serve the Confederacy by staying on his plantation and raising provisions. But Tom was not to be dissuaded. He joined the army on June 29, 1861, following his election as captain of the Haywood Highlanders. He and his men were mustered into state service as Company F of the 25th Regiment of North Carolina Infantry.

Unlike Walter, Tom left no record spelling out why he wanted to fight. As one of the leading landlords and slaveholders in a poor mountain county, he felt that it was his duty to set an example of leadership in war as he had in peace. He also realized that his neighbors expected no less of him. Laura indicated as much when she vainly pleaded with him to find the "moral courage to resist the importunities of those who wish to enlist under you." But Tom was not one to shun the burdens of leadership, whether in disciplining his slaves, morally uplifting his tenants, or commanding troops in defense of his community. Since following his father's wishes by moving out to Haywood, he had expected little from his life and entered the war with no illusions of glamour or adventure. His business interests would probably all be "a *wash up*" by the time he came back, he realized. But it hardly mattered. "It seems to me as if I can't do any thing or study or learn any thing—& consequently am getting along slowly with all my business."

Tom asked Rufus to join him in the Haywood Highlanders, but Rufus would have none of it and sat out the entire war at Fort Defiance. As the only adult male Lenoir residing at the home plantation, Rufus could justify his decision as being in the family's best interests; a trusted male figure had to supervise the family's core agricultural operations and financial dealings. As the youngest of the Lenoir children, Rufus had grown up under the shadow of his older brother William's wild mood swings. William's bewildering behavior taught Rufus as a child to seek order and security. He alone of the Lenoir brothers expressed no desire to strike out on bold ventures. A comfortable life with his wife and children at Fort Defiance was the extent of his ambition, and from the start he viewed the South's bid for independence as a threat to that life and a portent of disaster. He would cling to his familiar local world and leave the soldiering to others.

But even at home, security often seemed uncertain. For all the enthusiasm and unanimity with which most local whites embraced the outbreak of war, disturbing signs of political apathy and social division also emerged. A pro-Confederate meeting at Wilkesboro on April 29 had yielded a disappointingly small number of volunteers and only a modest amount of money to equip them. More alarmingly, Rufus learned that a group of James Gwyn's white neighbors had set fire to his woodlands. Before the fire was contained, several dwellings were lost to the blaze. Resorting to arson was a common tactic of poor whites in their feuds with wealthy planters. Certain he knew who was responsible for the outrage, Gwyn organized a vigilance committee. It rounded up three men and, bypassing the local courts, tried and convicted the accused. Two of them, Obadiah Sprinkle and Milton Sparks, were sentenced to thirty-nine lashes on their bare backs, had their heads half shaved, and were packed off to jail. The third, Obadiah's son, was released but warned to leave the county. Gwyn had met the challenge to his authority, but his problems hardly went away. By volunteering for military service, Sprinkle and Sparks gained a quick release from jail. They had no intention of fighting, however. Apparently deserting at the first opportunity, they were back in Wilkes County by late fall and free to exploit the unrest on the Confederate home front.

Although pleased with the record of Confederate armies in the early months of the war, Gwyn continued to worry about the level of support for the war. His doubts eased in July when a Union army was routed at Manassas, Virginia, but they soon returned. "I am sorry to find our common people so hard to arouse on the subject of trying to aid our noble soldiers in their patriotic cause," he wrote Rufus in October. Robina Norwood, a Lenoir cousin in the mountain town of Waynesville, also noted the apathy. A second call for volunteers in Waynesville had almost been "in vain," she reported. When her brothers rushed to volunteer in the spring, Robina had dared hope for a short war; by the fall, she was resigned to a long war that would be "both hard and onerous."

The war Robina had come to accept was the one Walter had always expected. He had a good sense from his travels in the North of the numbers and economic resources of the Union enemy as well as its commitment to fight. Still, Walter never wavered in his conviction that the Confederacy would triumph. What steeled his confidence was his belief in the righteousness of the Confederate cause. "Whatever may be our fate the cause for which we fight is just and righteous and must prevail," he wrote as he left to join Tom's unit.

Tom was waiting down in coastal South Carolina, hardly the military posting that he or his fellow mountaineers had expected. Recruiting had dried up after June, and the Highlanders made up the smallest company in the 25th North Carolina regiment. Tom and his men spent the summer waiting to be equipped with arms and learning how to become soldiers at Camp Clingman on the outskirts of Asheville, the largest town in the mountains. Most of their time was taken up with endless drills designed to teach them the intricacies of tactical formations on the battlefield. An even more valuable lesson was their indoctrination into taking military orders. A majority of the recruits were single young men barely out of their adolescence, unaccustomed to taking orders from anybody but their parents. Some rebelled against submitting to a discipline that they associated with the fawning dependence of slaves, but the ringleaders were arrested and the rebellion ended quickly.

Transferred in the fall to Raleigh and then Wilmington, the Highlanders were rushed to the South Carolina coast in response to the Union navy's seizure on November 7 of Port Royal, South Carolina, midway between Charleston and Savannah. Although Port Royal served for the rest of the war as the main base for the Union's South Atlantic blockading squadron, Federal forces were unable to push outward from Port Royal into the interior. Tom's company was part of the mobile defense system the Confederacy deployed to block any Federal advance. Positioned along the rail line running between Charleston and Savannah, Confederate reinforcements were poised to move quickly to attack the Federals once they tried to move inland, away from the protection of their naval guns. In explaining to Rufus how the flexible system was designed to work, Tom concluded that the Federals would stay on the coast and that skirmishing was likely the only fighting in store for him and his men. He was right. Little fighting occurred, and the greatest threat to the Confederates came from the bad water and unhealthy conditions of the marshy Carolina low country. Chills, fevers, and typhoid were rampant, adding to the misery of men coping with a measles epidemic, a childhood disease that struck when young men from isolated farms were packed together in military camps. At any given time during the first month of their service on the South Carolina coast, one-third of Tom's men were on the sick list.

Tom had been stationed at Camp Lee near Grahamville for two months when Walter finally joined him in early January 1862. Before leaving Fort Defiance on December 31, Walter compiled a list of his property holdings and personal notes for Rufus to use in paying his taxes, or, if he were killed in the war, as an aid in settling his estate. Ten slaves and a thousand acres of land in Watauga County comprised the bulk of his holdings. His own debts were small, the largest being the $771 that he owed Rufus; but as an endorser on the notes of local wealthy planters, he was potentially liable for over $6,000 more. With a lawyer's eye for detail, he carefully noted that his subscription to the Raleigh *Register* ran through April 13, 1862. Although he seemingly had thought of everything, he could not bring himself to do what his mother and sisters felt mattered more than anything else make a public profession of his Christian faith. He tried, but what he called "this rebellious frame of heart" held him back. He consoled himself with the hope that the war would teach him the Christian humility he had never experienced as a civilian. "While learning the duties of a soldier," he wrote in his journal, "I will try to conquer myself."

Walter's initiation into the life of a Confederate soldier got off to a rocky start when he reported to Camp Lee and attached himself to Tom's company. Fatigued after his trip and unaccustomed to camp food, he immediately came down with a cold and a "bilious derangement" that left him so woozy he had to withdraw from his first drill to keep from fainting. After taking two of the antibilious pills his mother had packed for him and a healthy dose of calomel (a laxative that was also used to expel intestinal worms), he felt better and adjusted to the routines of camp life. His greatest challenge came in learning how to drill.

Its commands and maneuvers were utterly foreign to him, and his fellow soldiers, mostly twelve-month enlistees who expected to be back home in the spring, had little interest in explaining them to a raw recruit they would soon be taking leave of. Since his officers were similarly indifferent, Walter had to teach himself by studying a borrowed copy of a drilling manual.

Walter had plenty of time to learn his drills. Aside from some probes up navigable rivers, the Yankees were content with shelling Confederate pickets and sending out reconnoitering parties of cavalry. When they were not drilling, the bored, restless Confederates whiled away the time by playing cards, competing in makeshift athletic games, and dancing and singing in two log houses they erected. Thanks to abundant supplies of corn, sweet potatoes, bacon, and beef from the plantations surrounding Camp Lee, they had plenty to eat. Making life even easier for the soldiers were the slaves who wandered through the camp selling molasses and vegetables and gathering up laundry to wash when they returned to their quarters in the outlying plantations.

After observing the slaves who came into the camp, Walter was pleased to report to Rufus that "the negroes about here seem humble & contented." Then, as if to calm Rufus's fears (if not his own as well) regarding the behavior of the slaves during the war, he added, "This does not look as their treachery would be thought very formidable, in case they were disposed to cooperate with the Yankees." Had Walter talked directly with the panic-stricken planters who fled inland after the Port Royal invasion, he might have arrived at a more ominous conclusion. The slaves had taken over their masters' abandoned plantations in joyful anticipation of the arrival of the Yankee soldiers.

A month of drilling, physical exercise, and eating meals cooked by Uriah, a slave Tom had brought with him from Haywood, left Walter feeling stronger and healthier than ever before. No one in his family had expected Walter, the frailest of the Lenoir brothers, to stand up to the physical demands of a soldier's life. Thus it was with pride that he wrote his mother that "I am increasing in weight by the development of my muscles of arms and legs, which are growing perceptibly larger and harder." Were it not for the inescapable dirt and grime, he would have been positively enjoying his days in the camp.

Elsewhere Federal forces were on the move. In early February 1862, an amphibious expedition led by General Ambrose E. Burnside gained a beachhead for Union forces in eastern North Carolina by seizing Roanoke Island, which controlled the channel between Pamlico and Albemarle sounds, the outlet to the Atlantic for all North Carolina ports except Wilmington. At the same time, a Union offensive in the west seized Forts Henry and Donelson in Tennessee and gained an entry point into the mid-South.

The military setbacks in February darkened Rufus's already gloomy take on the war. He had always looked to Walter for advice, and his older brother responded in February with the first in a series of letters aimed at shoring up his brother's morale. There was no reason to fear that a "just God" would abandon the South or indiscriminately punish the wicked in both the North and the South, he argued. God preferred to subdue wickedness not through punishment but through the manifestation of his infinite goodness and mercy. Walter depicted the Yankee soldiers as craven mercenaries who pillaged and terrorized defenseless white women and children in their barbaric war against the Confederacy. (This depiction of the Union foe was common in the Southern press from the first days of the war and was spread by the first returning wounded soldiers.) Surely, if any people deserved the scourge of divine wrath, it was the Yankees, not the Confederates. Soon their days of trial would come. To clinch his case, Walter rhetorically asked, "And then when we consider how right it is that we should be a free and independent nation & how wrong it would be for our foes to succeed in subjugating us, and in carrying out their wicked designs, how can we doubt that we have the aid of the overruling Providence that makes all things work together for final good?"

Repeating an argument he had jotted down in his war diary, Walter urged Rufus not to read too much into the recent Confederate reversals. Nothing vital had been lost, he argued. Although the loss of Forts Henry and Donelson did necessitate a Confederate withdrawal from Kentucky, Walter from the start had viewed the occupation of the state as "a blunder." The same was true, he believed, of the abortive Confederate military operations in the mountains of northwestern Virginia. As for the Federal incursion into eastern North Carolina, Walter predicted a "temporary success."

Rufus's greatest fear was that a Union victory in the war would reduce his family to homeless wanderers. Walter admitted that such a fate could not be ruled out, but he reminded Rufus that their grandfather had not been deterred by a similar prospect in taking up arms against the British at seemingly impossible odds. He advised his brother to seek solace in Psalms 37 and 56, with their promise to Christians that those who placed their trust in the Lord would live in peace and plentitude after their wicked oppressors were humbled.

The psalms were not enough. Rufus tried to shake his despondency, but he feared his brothers would come home in coffins. "I try hard," he wrote Tom and Walter in March, "to realize that you belong to your *country* and endeavor to wean my heart from you, and to think of *my* brothers on the same footing with my neighbor's brother but I *cannot*! We are all poor selfish creatures, and I am particularly so." He hoped that his faith in God would survive the "storms and breakers" the war would unleash and sustain him even if he lost all his property. He assured his brothers that he was no defeatist and had no thoughts of surrendering.

By the time Rufus's letter caught up with Tom and Walter, they were in eastern North Carolina, marching to block, if not turn back, a Union invasion led by General Burnside. Supported by a Federal fleet steaming up the Neuse River, Burnside moved out of his base on Roanoke Island, pushed through the Confederate defenses, and occupied New Bern on March 14.

In a trip that revealed the inadequacies of the Confederate rail system, Walter and the rest of the men in the North Carolina 25th spent four days on four different rail lines with three different gauges as they traveled from coastal South Carolina to the vicinity of Goldsboro, North Carolina, a distance of about 250 miles. After arriving in Charleston on the night of March 15, they marched from the depot of the Charleston & Savannah to that of the Northeastern Railroad, where the next morning they were to depart for Wilmington, North Carolina. Compared to the men spread out on the beds of open flat cars with side railings to keep them from rolling off, Tom and Walter enjoyed the comfort of traveling in boxcars, the sides of which they lined with their blankets to keep out the cold. Short one man who was killed when he fell from the top of a car, the troops made it to Goldsboro on the morning of March 18.

After shouting himself hoarse on the trip from "the excitement of moving towards the enemy," Walter was disappointed that his company was not immediately ordered into combat. As he told Rufus, "The 25th has been cruising round for a fight for a long time, but always has the luck to arrive a little too late." Still, he knew that his chance to prove himself in combat would come. "My mind is so made up," he insisted, "that I would be cheerful even in honorable captivity or exile, & that nothing would depress me but the thought of submission which I can't conceive that I will ever entertain."

Walter's best chance for combat came a week later, when part of his regiment was ordered south to Trenton to outflank a possible Union attempt to cut the rail line between Wilmington and Goldsboro. Although he saw no action in the end, he had marched eight miles loaded down by a knapsack, "a novel experiment to me & I stood it better than I expected." The personal satisfaction was readily apparent when he added, "I have roughed & toughed it out without additional care of myself or to exposure to weather &c." He might as well have said that frail Walter was becoming a man.

As military lines stabilized in eastern North Carolina, Walter had time to advise Rufus on how to cope with the uncertainties and price inflation of the Confederacy's wartime economy. The most pressing issue was whether Rufus should sell the lands in William's estate. Walter originally favored selling the lands as soon as possible while the improvements on them were still in good shape and prices were not depressed by the war. He changed his mind, however, when the Confederate money supply swelled in response to the lengthening war. The paper currency issued to finance the war, combined with stay laws that postponed the payment of individual debts, resulted in a rapidly expanding supply of money that was bound to drive up prices. Since it was now clear that William's lands would increase in value, at least in paper money, Walter urged Rufus to put off any sales. No one was paying in specie, so Rufus would have to accept paper currency, and then he would be left with the problem of what to do with it. The money could not be loaned out with any degree of security because knowledgeable investors would take advantage of money cheapened by inflation to pay off their debts rather than incur new ones. Foreseeing a collapse of prices and a return of tight money once the war was over, both of which would make it difficult to collect on debts, Walter cautioned Rufus against making any loans during the war.

As for Rufus's surplus funds, Walter recommended investing in cotton and slaves. Prices for both had dropped early in the war in response to the Union blockade and the falling demand for slaves as planters shifted land out of cotton into food crops. Reasoning that diminished supplies of cotton would soon drive up its price, as well as that of the slaves who produced it, Walter felt that both offered an excellent potential for long-range profits. He suggested that Rufus consider making his purchases where prices were the lowest—areas of the Confederacy under immediate threat of a Union attack—and then removing his cotton and slaves to a secure spot up in the mountains until the war was over. Recognizing that "for reasons, not pecuniary, you would be altogether averse to owning any more slaves than you are already responsible for," he pushed cotton speculation as the more comfortable course for Rufus to follow. Finally, Walter recommended purchasing the Confederate government's 8 percent bonds. They seemed "perhaps the safest" investment that Rufus could make for himself, his mother, and sister Sarah. The bonds could probably be bought at less than par, though Walter "would not be willing from patriotic motives to get them even as agent for another at too heavy a discount."

Anticipating Rufus's objection that Confederate bonds would be worthless if the Union won the war, Walter appealed to his brother's sense of honor and duty. If the Confederacy fell, he argued, what difference would the loss of a few bonds make? "Would any of us be willing to hold any of our property on the dishonorable and disgraceful terms, to ourselves and our remotest posterity, of submitting ourselves and our country to subjugation to a government not our own? For my part I have long since made up my mind to say, No." Walter insisted that "no amount of wealth" could make a true Southerner endure the "degradation" implied in submission to Yankee rule. Face up to your worst fears, he continued, and you will learn that you can still be happy without your wealth. Drawing on his experience as a soldier and assuming the tone of a Sunday preacher moralizing to the poor, Walter pointed out that hard work and physical fatigue only heightened the pleasure of a coarse meal or a night's rest on a hard surface. Happiness came from within, not from material goods. If Rufus and his family "lost in this struggle all but your lives, and the knowledge that you had been true to your duty and your country, you, as well as I, could in some other land have before us an undiminished prospect for a contented, cheerful, happy life."

Walter was eager to shore up his brother's patriotism because of some disturbing information passed to him in camp. Rufus had initially balked at accepting Confederate paper money in payment of a debt owed him by the Patterson cotton factory in Caldwell County. As a result, his patriotism was called into question, and he faced heavy local criticism. Walter agreed that like any "prudent property holder" Rufus had every right to hold out for a more secure form of payment. Still, with so many sacrificing on behalf of the Confederate cause, it was only natural that willingness to accept the government's money was a sensitive issue. Suspecting that Rufus's personal enemies were exploiting the incident to undermine his local influence, Walter urged his brother to set himself "right" by seizing the first opportunity to proclaim his patriotism.

In April 1862, Tom Lenoir decided to leave the army at the end of his twelve-month enlistment. A bad cold he caught on the train trip to Goldsboro left him with a hacking cough, and he was too weak to participate in company drills. He was also worried by the news he was receiving from his overseer in Haywood. Local whites had been stealing bacon from Tom's smokehouse, and tenants had slackened off in meeting their rental payments of corn. In addition, many mountain folk were up in arms over the Confederate draft just passed, and a "rebellion" was feared. Tom concluded that this was all the more reason to head back home.

Tom, now forty-four years old, was free to leave the army because the Confederate Conscription Act passed in April 1862 only covered men up to the age of thirty-five. All men between eighteen and thirty-five were drafted for three years (or less if the war ended sooner), including those who had volunteered at the start of the war and whose enlistments would have expired in the spring of 1862. It was this feature of the draft that the men already in the army most resented. Although Walter felt their grievances were valid, he had nothing but contempt for the "evil disposed persons" circulating through his camp stirring up insubordination among the men. The best way to deal with the grumbling, he suggested, would be to send some of the disaffected men home and "let them & the rest of the army see how the women at home would hate them and despise them and loathe them."

With Tom gone, Walter accepted an offer to serve as an officer in a Caldwell company under recruitment for Vance's Legion, a hybrid military unit that combined three regiments with some attached cavalry and artillery. On April 28 Walter left his camp near Kinston, North Carolina, and headed to Caldwell to assist in the recruiting.

Only four months had passed since Walter had left to join Tom, but the strains of the war were evident in Caldwell and the other western counties of North Carolina. Provisions were short, prices high, and the poor reduced to begging for such essentials as salt. Even the planters were having difficulty in getting the salt they needed, an inconvenience Rufus characterized as "only one drop from the bucket of bitter calamities to be poured over our land." The planters did their best to distribute any food surpluses they had, but many were as discouraged as James Gwyn, who complained about the grain converted to whiskey in the numerous stills of the local farmers. The growing casualty lists also sapped morale. "I scarcely know a home that is not desolated by this fearful war," one relative wrote in February.

For all the hardships on the home front, support for the war was still strong enough in the spring of 1862 to allow the original companies raised in Caldwell to easily refill their ranks. Avoidance of the stigma of being drafted and the desire to bond with friends and relatives who had been the first to enlist played a major role in drawing older men into the army. But at least as important was the fear of being seen as an effeminate coward by the young women, nearly all of whom were impassioned Confederates. In addition to sewing and weaving clothes for the troops and sending off packages of food, household items, and bandages, young women served as the Confederate army's most effective recruiters. Laura Norwood, Walter's twenty-one-year niece, took pride in referring to herself as a "little rebel." She was among the young women who presented a company flag to the Caldwell Rough and Readys when they left Lenoir for the war. Writing Walter in April 1862, she assured him that "never will *I be defeated, never*, under the Sun!" For her and countless other young women, the war was a heroic adventure in which the "generous, the brave, the self denying, self-forgetting, the fearless, the true-hearted, the daring, the unyielding to temptation, in a word the *True!*" risked all in the defense of their country and loved ones. She need hardly have added that no coward could ever claim her love.

Even Confederates who did not share Laura's romanticized view of the war found reason enough to steel themselves when they read or heard of Yankee atrocities committed on Southern soil. It was this image of the Yankees as vile criminals, not any positive measures of the Confederate government, which sustained morale in former Union counties such as Caldwell. Unlike Laura, Walter's sister Sarah was a reluctant Confederate at the onset of what she called this "cruel war." But her nephew Nathan Gwyn, home recuperating from a wound in the winter of 1862, convinced her of the need to endure whatever sacrifices were called for. "It makes my heart ache and my blood boil to hear Nathan tell about those Yankees!" she wrote Walter. "I could not believe the newspapers! But I have to believe him! Surely our army would not do so, in the Northern States. They would not harm the women and children and destroy the churches!"

Confederates were especially enraged in the spring of 1862 when General Benjamin F. Butler occupied New Orleans. Angered by the scorn the women of the city heaped upon his soldiers, Butler issued an order on May 5, 1862, declaring that any woman who insulted Federal soldiers should be "regarded and held liable to be treated as a woman of the town plying her trade." Reprinted in bold type on the front page of newspapers across the South, Butler's order was universally denounced as an unconscionable insult to Southern women and an assault on their sexual purity. In the minds of Southerners, Butler had placed himself beyond the pale of any shred of decency. Walter's niece Louise Norwood was typical in her venomous outrage: "I wish some negro would kill him for soap-grease." Walter said much the same when he wrote Rufus that "I would kill the wretch, if I could, with more pleasure than I would destroy a hyena or centipede."

Whatever civilian grumblings Walter might have detected in Caldwell did not shake his faith in a Confederate victory. In his diary he professed the belief that the "Southern people are more than ever, intensely united and in earnest." What gains the Union army had achieved had come at a great and, to Walter, unsustainable cost. If the Confederacy could hold its ground and turn back the two great Union offenses in Virginia and Tennessee, he foresaw recognition and independence by the summer of 1862.

After two weeks of recruiting for the Caldwell Riflemen, Walter left Lenoir on May 15 for Kinston, North Carolina, the staging area for the companies of Vance's Legion. Recruiting for his new company had been spotty, and it reached its required strength only by taking surplus recruits from the two other companies in Caldwell. In the company elections Walter was chosen first lieutenant. Although upset with the election of Thomas Dula as captain, whom he considered unfit for the responsibility, Walter accepted his office out of a sense of duty to the men he had asked to join him in the new company. Weighed down by the responsibilities and cares of an officer, he doubted that he would enjoy his military service as much as he had as a private. He had no ambition to rise in the army, only an unyielding determination to accept any assignment in pursuit of Confederate independence.

On May 26, Walter arrived at Camp Vance, near Kittrell's Springs in Granville County. Despite its healthy location in a thicket of pines with access to good water, the camp from the beginning was a breeding ground of discontent. Many of Vance's fellow officers did not share his exaggerated opinion of his fighting abilities at the battle of New Bern, and neither did the authorities in Raleigh and Richmond. Knowing that the Confederate War Department now considered legions too cumbersome to be deployed effectively on the battlefield, state officials gave Vance no support in his recruiting efforts. Nor did Vance's commanding officer authorize him to leave camp on a recruiting mission. As a result, Vance failed to raise enough men for his legion in the thirty days allotted after the passage of the Confederate draft in April. In the meantime, the soldiers who did assemble at Camp Vance were in limbo. They had rations to eat and plank shanties for their quarters but no camp equipment. They had no arms, no medical officer, and no field officer to take charge of their training.

Tired of waiting to learn the fate of their legion, many men simply packed up and headed home. Rather than tightening discipline, most of the company officers responded by being generous in their furloughs. Of the four companies that showed up at Camp Vance, only Walter's and another were still present for duty in late June. In the absence of the "fickle and unreliable" Captain Dula, who was off trying to find a place for his orphan company, Walter did his best to hold his company together and maintain discipline. When eight of his men started home without leave, Walter ordered out the cavalry to bring them back. The only furloughs he granted were to men on the sick list. Since no medical officers had been provided, he relied on home remedies passed on by his mother and Laura Norwood to deal with most common complaints. To head off a fever, there was salt and vinegar; for the "flux" (diarrhea) tea brewed from pepper weed. To boast morale, he encouraged hymn singing. He had enjoyed doing so as a boy, and now, knowing that he would need a strong, clear voice to issue commands, he joined in with gusto "to exercise my lungs and voice, which I regard as very important to me."

In late June, Walter took a break from his camp duties and went to Richmond to confer with Vance on the disposition of the men in his Caldwell company. There he had a chance to walk over the sites of the Seven Days Battles, where thousands of Confederate troops had successfully defended Richmond against General George B. McClellan's massive Union army. The signs of combat were still fresh and raw when Walter visited on June 30, picking up spent bullets, Yankee cartridges, and other battlefield detritus as souvenirs for Rufus. He was struck by the incongruity of seeing so many dead and dying soldiers covering placid farm fields: "To the eye they were fields with the fences down, the crops less interfered with than you would have supposed, and fresh graves and dead men & horses lying in the sun, here & there, all over them." When he returned a few days later to sites he had already visited, he observed that many of the Yankee dead were still unburied. One poor soul, a wounded Yankee whom Walter had seen on Monday, was still there on Friday, "dying but not yet dead." By then, the Confederate dead had found a resting place in shallow graves dug where they fell, their names inscribed on crude pieces of planking placed at the heads of their graves. Unless the bodies were removed to a new burial site and more permanent markings erected, the identity of the fallen would be forever lost, he mused. "They fell fighting as heroes and patriots fight," he wrote Rufus, "and they will be remembered and thought of with love & regret at home, long after their memory would have been forgotten if they had lived in inglorious ease at home."

Although Rufus was among those who chose to stay at home, Walter honored his brother's commitment to provide for and to protect the Lenoirs and their family interests at Fort Defiance. Among those interests was the money Rufus collected from Walter's debtors. When George Harper paid off a large loan with

This was the scene confronting a burial detail of Union soldiers after the battle of Fair Oaks during the Peninsula Campaign. The crotched sticks had been used to support tents at a Union campsite.

Confederate paper money in the spring, Walter repeated what he had advised Rufus earlier: convert the money into cotton and slaves, both of which were cheap and likely to rise in value. Walter still described himself as a slave owner "against my will," but, he explained to Rufus, "I would rather buy some negroes at say half the former highest prices, than run the risk of keeping so much paper money."

Tom joined his brothers in cotton speculation soon after he returned from the army. He had set aside $1,500 to buy several bales of cotton that he stored in up-country South Carolina as a reserve to tap at the end of the war, when he expected prices would be much higher. He brought a bale back with him for his own use and another that he planned to give away to the families of the local volunteers. Cotton goods were now scarce in the mountains, and to meet the local demand Tom placed an order with Rufus for cotton yard and bolts of cloth from the factory in Patterson. Much of this he intended to distribute to the soldiers' families, especially those with kin in Tom's old company that had suffered heavy casualties in the fighting around Richmond.

Meanwhile, Walter learned that Vance's Legion was being disbanded. Walter was left with two unappealing choices. He could join Captain Dula and most of the company and be attached to General Kirby Smith's army in East Tennessee. Worse, he could be sent to guard Union prisoners at Salisbury, North Carolina, an assignment Walter felt "would bring reproach" on himself and the company. He was on the verge of resigning his lieutenancy and attaching himself as a private to any unit likely to see fighting in the main eastern theater in Virginia when he was surprised to hear on July 23 that he had been elected and appointed first lieutenant of Company A in the 37th North Carolina regiment. He jumped at the opportunity.

On the way to Richmond, Walter learned that the captain of Company A had resigned on account of bad health, and he had been promoted to take the captain's place. The news left him with a heavy sense of responsibility, for he was now being asked to command battle-hardened veterans. The anxieties that had plagued him as a college student and struggling young lawyer returned. "Will I again grow negligent & slothful and forgetful" or use my new post as an excuse for "procrastinating the discharge of the solemn duties of religion?" he asked himself in his diary. But "hard study and constant diligence" would pull him through, he decided, so long as he remained in good health.

After months of inactivity, the prospect of battle exhilarated him. "If I live to see you afterwards," he wrote Rufus, "I will perhaps be able to tell you that I have been in the grandest battle ever fought in America, one of the grandest ever fought in the world." In writing his mother, he was careful to stress that he was experiencing "an increased concern on the subject of my religious condition, and a nearer approach towards a willingness to connect myself with the church." Were he to survive the "rough side of war" and meet her once more "in this world," he assured her that "in that one moment I will be amply rewarded for it all." If they did not meet, he reminded her that a death in battle would be an honorable one and that he had arranged all his affairs before leaving for the army with that contingency in mind. "I would leave no one unprovided for depending immediately on me for a sustaining hand, and would I hope leave no stain on the good name I had inherited. I would die in a just cause, and, I am very sure, in a struggle that will secure us ultimate triumph."

Selina accepted her son's decision with the resignation of a Christian mother who trusted in God's will. She wrote in response that Walter's absence from home had made the whole family realize "how necessary you were to the happiness of us all." Still, she hastened to add, she had done her duty in giving up a son for "the good of my country." She urged Walter to pray, as she would, for his safety, and cautioned him to keep taking his antibilious pills to ward off jaundice and stomach ailments.

Walter spent his first night in Richmond sleeping on the pavement outside the depot of the Virginia Central Railroad waiting for a train in the morning to Gordonsville, Virginia. Lincoln had ordered McClellan's army back to Washington in late July, so Walter's new regiment, part of Branch's brigade in A. P. Hill's division, headed north to help counter the threat of Union General John Pope's Army of Virginia marching southward from Washington.

Walter's regiment had been in camp near Gordonsville for only a few days when it received marching orders on August 6. As he began the march, he worried that his churning stomach might force him to fall to the rear with a bout of diarrhea. But his stomach calmed as he trudged along with his heavy knapsack, and he found himself relishing the nightly fare of dry army crackers, cakes of flour heated on strips of wood over an open fire, badly cooked beef roasted on sticks, and raw bacon. After a few days he and his men were filthy and covered with body lice, an indignity Walter blamed on the abandoned Yankee knapsacks they found on the outskirts of Richmond. "As for being dirty," he wrote Rufus with a soldier's detachment, "we are past caring for that, & we can even think of being lousy as a military necessity to be submitted to cheerfully when it can be no longer avoided." The hardest march came on August 9 and many of the men, including the only other commissioned officer in Walter's company, fell out of the ranks. A battle was developing twelve miles ahead, and on a hot, sunny day their commanders were rushing them forward as reinforcements. Since learning that he would be serving in General Thomas "Stonewall" Jackson's corps, Walter had always expected to be sent "to some place where there is good work to be done." That place was Cedar Mountain.

The men were exhausted when they reached the battle raging near Culpeper on the north side of the Rapidan River. The most prominent topographical feature of the battle site was Cedar Mountain, and the Confederates spent most of the afternoon trying to occupy its ridges in order to position themselves to turn the Federal left flank. Concealed from their view, Union troops massed in a thick woods and rolling fields of wheat and corn. Ordered forward late in the afternoon, these troops caught the Confederates by surprise, broke through a brigade of Virginians, and sent them reeling back in retreat. Only the timely arrival of the reinforcements from A. P. Hill's division prevented a Confederate defeat.

Walter's company had about an hour to rest before it was thrown into the battle to fill the gap in the Confederate lines. As the moment of decision approached, he experienced less of the

Cedar Mountain looms in the background as Union troops prepare to move against the Confederate lines.
(SOURCE: *North Carolina Collection, Wilson Library, University of North Carolina–Chapel Hill.*)

"nervousness and timidity" he had felt when addressing a jury. The thought of dying, but not of being wounded, ran through his mind. Most of his men, he observed, became serious as they awaited battle, yet once in action they seemed to possess an amazing ability to cast aside their fear of death and face with cool indifference the awful sights and sounds that would envelop them. He described this ability as "one of the most marvelous things in human nature."

The battle enveloped Walter in a bedlam of noise and confusion as the retreating Virginians swarmed through the Confederate lines, separating him from some of the men in his company. As an officer, Walter was on his own, and was able to keep the remnant of his company moving forward only by constant effort. After pressing through the woods in pursuit of the Yankees now visible in the trees, the Confederates regrouped behind a fence bordering the road running north to Culpeper. After reaching the fence, Walter went up and down the Confederate line searching for the rest of his company. To his relief, he found them in a washed-out cut along the road. He spoke to as many as he could, offering encouragement and helping some load their rifles. After repulsing a Union cavalry charge ("in almost an instant eight or ten dead horses were piled in the road"), the Confederates charged across the road and through a cornfield. With two of his men leaning on his shoulder for support, Walter led his men across the cornfield to attack the fleeing Yankees, but they quickly fell back to a safe position.

Under a moonlit sky, Walter's company bivouacked for the night in the middle of the cornfield surrounded by dead and dying Union soldiers. After praising his men for their bravery and checking on casualties and those present for duty, Walter joined other Confederates in roaming over the battlefield. As he did so, he marveled over the contrast in casualties. The Yankees had been badly bloodied; Walter had stepped over the bodies of at least six or eight of their dead. Yet no one had been killed or wounded in Walter's company and casualties in his regiment were very light. He could find no explanation for the contrast "except that our God in whom we trust favored our righteous cause."

The day after the battle, a cold rain fell, and Walter was soaked when he made camp after a six-mile march. Stonewall Jackson was not to be stopped by the previous day's skirmish. He drove the brigade forward, toward a rendezvous with Pope's army at Manassas. Walter snatched a few hours sleep after picket duty and awoke the next day to wring out the wet socks he had slept in. He was amazed that he was still cheerful under conditions that would have made him miserable as a civilian, a circumstance he took to be another sign that "God is on our side in this war." Indeed, days of hard marches and sleeping in the damp air had left him feeling stronger than when he had reported for duty in Richmond. He would need all that strength in the coming weeks.

In the last days of August 1862, the Confederate and Union forces once again clashed in the vicinity of Manassas Junction, Virginia. Walter's company saw its heaviest fighting on August 29, the first day of the battle. Jackson had drawn up his army behind an abandoned railroad right-of-way fronted by pockets of heavy forest about a mile west of the site of the First Battle of Bull Run. Early in the afternoon Pope launched a series of uncoordinated attacks against the Confederate lines. The heaviest fell against the Confederate left flank defended by A. P. Hill's division and the

North Carolina 37th. A few minutes after they entered the battle early in the afternoon, two-thirds of the men in Walter's Company A had been killed or wounded. As at Cedar Mountain, Walter concentrated on herding his men back into line. More than once, he had to seize men by the shoulders and force them to hold their ground. His company made its first stand in part of the railroad cut. In the confusion and smoke Walter heard a bullet whiz by his ear. As he instinctively turned away, he saw William Weaver, a soldier in his company, dead at his feet. The bullet that just missed Walter had blown though Weaver's head. Walter was forever haunted by what he saw: the dead Weaver "seemed to look me in the face with an expression I cannot forget, a gentle smile on his lips and a look from the eyes that seemed to ask me for aid."

Despite Walter's efforts, his company fell back when the men noticed that supporting Confederates on either side of them had retreated. After reluctantly joining his company, which had regrouped fifty yards in the rear, Walter exhorted his men to return to the battle. Until nightfall they coolly withstood Federal attacks across the railroad cut. The Confederate lines had held, and the arrival of General James B. Longstreet's corps on the afternoon of August 29 ensured that the Confederates would drive the Yankees from the battlefield in the fighting on August 30.

Walter's men rested on August 30, as Pope's army pulled back toward Washington. On Sunday, Walter walked over the ground where his company had fought two days earlier. He used his knife to pry a minie ball (the common term for the Minié ball, an elongated bullet created by a French army captain that was used in Civil War rifled muskets) from the bark of a hickory tree. Walter had been standing by that tree on Friday when the ball that just

Comparable to Walter's haunting memory of the dead William Weaver is this image of a soldier killed in the Petersburg trenches in the last days of the war. (SOURCE: *Library of Congress, Prints & Photographs Division, LC-USZC4-1850.*)

missed him smashed through Weaver's head. He crossed over to the railroad cut where his company had been in the thick of the fighting and noted that all the trees had been struck several times by minie balls. At one white oak, not much wider than a man's body, he counted where twenty balls had hit. He wondered how any of his men survived.

When he was able to resume his diary months later, Walter noted that he "had desired from the first to be in one battle, partly from curiosity, and partly because I wished to know and feel, if I had survived the war, that I had done some thing on the battle field to maintain the independence of my country." Cedar

Mountain had satisfied that curiosity and he had "no *desire* to see another battle." But Walter continued to fight out of a sense of duty, and the killing fields of Second Manassas were far more harrowing than what he encountered at Cedar Mountain. As he left the sobering scene where Weaver had stared up at him with a dead man's plea for help, Walter had no idea that he and his men would be in an even hotter fight the very next day. In that battle Walter's good fortune ran out.

NOTES

The standard account of secession in North Carolina remains J. Carlyle Sitterson, *The Secession Movement in North Carolina* (Chapel Hill: University of North Carolina Press, 1939), but it should be supplemented with the innovative statistical analysis in Daniel W. Crofts, *Reluctant Confederates: Upper South Unionists in the Secession Crisis* (Chapel Hill: University of North Carolina Press, 1989). A brief overview of the secession campaigns in the Southern states can be found in Ralph A. Wooster, *The Secession Conventions of the South* (Princeton: Princeton University Press, 1962). For reactions in the North and contrasting views on efforts in Congress to defuse the crisis, see David M. Potter, *Lincoln and His Party in the Secession Crisis* (New Haven: Yale University Press, 1942); and Kenneth M. Stampp, *And the War Came: The North and the Secession Crisis, 1860–1861* (Baton Rouge: Louisiana State University Press, 1950).

The letters in the Lenoir Family Papers reveal how shocked the Lenoirs and their friends were over the suddenness and severity of the crisis. The fullest expression of Walter's views can be found in the exchange of letters between Walter and Zebulon Vance included in Frontis W. Johnston, ed., *The Papers of Zebulon Baird Vance*, vol. 1, *1843–1862* (Raleigh: North Carolina Department of Archives and History, 1963). Crofts, *Reluctant Confederates*, pp. 314–15, 329, 332–33, provides the best account of the near unanimity with which Unionists in the Upper South blamed Lincoln and his calling for troops for touching off the war.

For the military side of the war, James M. McPherson, *Battle Cry of Freedom: The Civil War Era* (New York: Oxford University Press, 1988) is unsurpassed for its clear narrative flow. More detailed is Russell F. Weigley, *A Great Civil War: A Military and Political History, 1861–1865* (Bloomington: Indiana University Press, 2000). John G. Barrett, *The Civil War in North Carolina* (Chapel Hill: University of North Carolina Press, 1963) covers the war in North Carolina.

Walter's account of his conversion to the Confederate cause is found in his wartime letter to Rufus on September 27, 1863. The details on Walter's initiation into Confederate military service and his reaction to army life and combat come from his wartime diary, the original and a typescript version that are in the Lenoir Family Papers. The diary begins with an entry on January 14, 1862, soon after he arrived at Grahamville, South Carolina. For conditions in the Confederate camps, see the wonderfully readable account in Bell Irvin Wiley, *The Life of Johnny Reb: The Common Soldier of the Confederacy* (Indianapolis: Bobbs-Merrill, 1943). Paul E. Steiner, *Disease in the Civil War: Natural Biological Warfare in 1861–1865* (Springfield, Ill.: Thomas, 1968), explains why the debilitating outbreaks of disease noted by Walter were so common throughout the Civil War among soldiers.

The last entry in Walter's diary for 1862 was on July 27, two days before he was swept up in Lee's counteroffensive against Pope's Union army. John J. Hennessy, *Return to Bull Run: The Campaign and Battle of Second Manassas* (New York: Simon & Schuster, 1993) offers a superb account of the ensuing campaign.

· *Three* ·

AGONY AT OX HILL

‑‑‑⁓‑‑‑

A‌FTER THAT TERRIBLE MAULING ON FRIDAY AT MANASSAS Junction, Walter and the fifteen men in his company still fit for duty (out of around fifty who went north as part of Jackson's corps) could have been forgiven if they thought they had earned a rest. But Lee hoped to deliver a knockout blow against Pope's army, the bulk of which had withdrawn by August 31 to Centreville astraddle a road that led back to the safety of the Washington defenses. Lee ordered Jackson on a circling maneuver intended to place him at Fairfax Court House, eight miles behind Pope's army on its line of retreat to Washington. If the maneuver succeeded, Pope's retreat would be blocked and he would have to come out in the open and fight. However, the element of surprise was lost when a Union patrol detected Jackson's move around Pope's right flank. As Pope hurriedly redeployed his army toward Fairfax, Yankees coming up from the south attacked the advanced units of Jackson's corps at the crossroads of Chantilly, a site also known as Ox Hill.

The battle began around 5:00 P.M. and was fought in a raging thunderstorm. Walter's company was in the thick of the sharpest engagement at Ox Hill, and he was proud of how his small band was fighting. Later he learned that only three of his men escaped from that battle unwounded. In the two hours of the heaviest fighting they and fellow Carolinians charged across a field, pushed the Federals though woods into another field, and then held back Union counterattacks at the edge of the woods. After two Union generals were killed in rapid succession, the Federals called off the attacks in the gathering darkness.

It was twilight, Walter recalled, and time for a rest. The battle seemed to be winding down. On a slight ridge behind a fence line he was resting on the ground. Leaning back on an elbow, he foolishly stretched out his legs across the line of fire rather than pointing them to the rear. He had just finished talking with Captain Morris and was about to speak to his men when he felt an "awful pain" in his right leg. A minie ball had ripped through it about halfway between his knee and foot, smashing both bones. No sooner had he told Morris that he thought his leg was broken when a second ball, perhaps skipping up from the ground, laid bare the shinbone in the same leg and took off his right toe. Disabled and fearing that he would bleed to death from a severed artery, he began to drag himself toward the rear in the frantic hope of finding members of an infantry corps. Exhausted after crawling for about fifteen feet, he collapsed in a small clearing by the road. As sand was thrown into his face by minie balls striking the ground near his head and Yankee artillery shells exploded all around him, he realized that he was in a more exposed position than the fence line he had just left. He lay hopeless, waiting to die.

Looking back, Walter marveled at how calm and resigned he had felt. What sustained him was faith in the God he never had

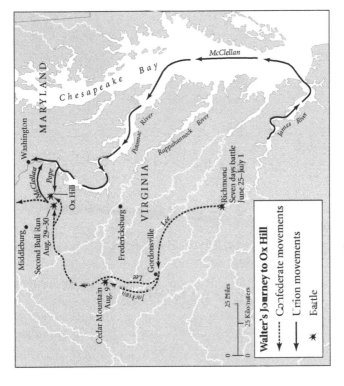

Walter's journey to Ox Hill.

On the morning of August 31, the day Walter was wounded, Pope's army regrouped in Centreville.
(SOURCE: *Library of Congress, Prints & Photographs Division, LC-USZC4-3259.*)

acknowledged in a public confession of faith. He felt that he was "in the hands of a good and merciful God and that he would do with me what was right." His mind wandered. He experienced a strange sense of elation when he realized that he was not about to lose one of his arms. Surely, it would be more convenient to have a leg rather than an arm amputated. Or would it? What about his favorite sport of trout fishing or the other outdoor activities he would have to give up? He fantasized about women and whether he ever again would have sexual relations. True, he had abstained since Nealy's death, but would he do so in the future out of a sense of inadequacy? Elation gave way to sadness, for he "was not old enough to have given up the thought of a woman. Are men ever?" Sadness then gave way to shame for harboring such "poor unworthy thoughts," musings on

Battlefield of "Chantilly."

Walter was wounded while resting behind the fence in the foreground of this 1907 view of the field where he and his men fought at Ox Hill. (SOURCE: *Virginia Room, Fairfax County Public Library.*)

"mere enjoyments," when he should have been thankful for being alive.

Just after dark, one of Walter's men came across him lying in a bloody heap, soaked by the falling rain. More help arrived, and four Confederates lifted Walter onto a makeshift stretcher put together by draping a blanket over two fence rails. As they moved him, the pain was agonizing, and he allowed himself to scream out for the first time. He was carried in the dark about a quarter of a mile to a farmhouse where he was left, along with several other wounded men, on the narrow front porch. It was so crowded by the time they arrived with Walter that the only available space was at the entryway to the house. Throughout the night he experienced the "great torture" of having his wounded leg inadvertently kicked by Confederate

Like Walter after the battle at Ox Hill, these wounded
Union soldiers in Virginia had to wait their turn for
medical treatment.
(Source: *Francis Trevelyn Miller, ed.,* The Photo-
graphic History of the Civil War, vol. 8, *New York:*
Thomas Yoseloff, 1959, p. 255.)

personnel entering and leaving the house. In the morning he was
carried about three-quarters of a mile on a stretcher to an old field
where a temporary hospital had been set up. Walter had to wait his
turn along with several others. Finally, at about ten o'clock on the
morning of September 3, some forty hours after he had been shot, he
looked up to see a team of surgeons hovering over him.

Dr. John F. Shaffner of the 33rd North Carolina Regiment
headed up the team. His treatment for the wound was a foregone
conclusion. Amputation was the only option in treating the vast

majority of those wounded by minie balls. Large and heavy at a .58-caliber and relatively slow moving, the soft lead bullets of rifled muskets caused catastrophic injuries. Rather than blowing through a body, they plowed in and produced large, gaping holes as they smashed bones and tore apart muscles and tissues. No medical techniques existed to repair the damage, and amputation offered the best chance to arrest the spread of infection as tissues decayed, pus spread through the blood, and bone marrow swelled from inflammation. Wounds to the head, stomach, or chest were almost always fatal, and those wounded were treated last, if at all. At least Walter had been hit in an extremity, the most common battlefield wound. Army surgeons quickly gained experience in amputating an arm or a leg and survival rates were high.

Dr. Shaffner had an ample supply of chloroform, and Walter was blissfully unconscious during the ten minutes or so of the operation. Most likely, blood from previous operations splattered the doctor's uniform; the notion of sterile operations postdated the Civil War. Shaffner began by washing out the wound with a sponge or cloth that had been rinsed in cool water after being used on a previous patient. He then used his bare finger to probe the wound looking for debris and the bullet. Once he was certain that Walter was insensible from the chloroform, he made a series of incisions with his scalpel down to the bone, pulled away muscle and skin, and left a flap of skin on one side of the wound. The key decision was where to amputate. In Walter's case, it was about six inches below his right knee. Normally Schoeffner would have severed the leg with his bonesaw nearer to the knee joint, thereby allowing for an easier, less painful adjustment to a wooden leg in contact with a short stump. He decided not to out of concern that complications might arise were he to amputate at the point where the second minie ball had badly gouged Walter's shin just below his knee joint. He feared that the damaged shinbone might be so weakened after being cut through that it would be unable to bear the weight of a prosthetic device. Once the amputation was over and he had tossed the severed leg onto a nearby pile of limbs, Shaffner tied off Walter's arteries with horsehair or perhaps cloth threads. He then carefully scraped the remaining bone on the leg to prevent any sharp edges from pushing through the skin, pulled the flap of skin back across the wound, and sewed it up so as to leave a drainage hole. Just as he finished dressing the wound with

This Confederate field hospital at Antietam was typical of the emergency medical services provided for the wounded after a battle.
(SOURCE: *Library of Congress, Prints & Photographs Division, LC-DIG-cwpb-00202.*)

a medicinal plaster covered by a bandage, Walter regained consciousness. Little did he realize that his greatest agony lay ahead.

Within hours of surgery, Walter found himself in the bed of a heavy army wagon pressed into service as an ambulance. Accompanying him were Rufus Holdaway, a private from his company detailed as his nurse, and two friends, his nephew Tom Norwood and Lieutenant Pool. Tom had been shot in his left heel and Pool was still dazed from an exploding shell. Their destination was Middleburg in Loudoun County, Virginia, where a military hospital had been established in an Episcopal church. As the wagon rumbled off in midafternoon, Walter began the worst journey of his life. Equipped with no springs, the wagon did not so much carry him as it bounced him. Every bump on the rough farm road jarred his wound. As bad as the pain had been while he lay in the field waiting for the surgeons, this was infinitely worse. He later wrote that every little jolt of the wagon caused "a pang which felt as if my stump was thrust into liquid fire, and was as fierce as that awful pang which first announced that my leg was broken." Mercifully for Walter, the driver stopped at nightfall after covering twenty miles in about five hours. Just outside the village of Aldie and still four miles from Middleburg, the men spent the night in the bed of the wagon.

When their journey resumed, so did Walter's excruciating pain. He was convinced he was going to die. About three miles outside of Middleburg the men flagged down a passing Rockaway carriage, a horse-drawn passenger vehicle that had springs, which carried Walter into town with much less suffering.

Still ahead, however, was the problem of finding accommodations for himself and Tom. About 1,800 Confederate sick and wounded had flooded into Middleburg, and even if the military hospital in the church had not been packed, Walter would have done all in his power to avoid it. Understaffed and filled to overflowing, military hospitals were sites of agony and death. Walter wanted to rent a room in a private residence. Uncertain how to proceed, he waited alone and helpless in the Rockaway. A passerby, Mrs. Samuel A. Chancellor, noticed his plight and offered assistance. For Walter, she was a guardian angel. She spoke to him, he remembered, "in that sweet kind woman's voice that thrills the heart of the sufferer as nothing else can." Handled throughout his ordeal by well-meaning but rough men inured to suffering by the carnage they had seen, for the first time he "felt the soft touch of woman's hand," and he never forgot how "it soothed and comforted" him. Chancellor's house was already filled with the wounded, but she procured a room for Walter in the home of a Methodist clergyman, Reverend Richey.

Once settled, Walter wrote to Rufus. His pain was so intense that his trembling hand reduced his normally neat cursive script to the shaky block letters of a child. Not knowing what news or rumors Rufus may have heard, he began with the simple and reassuring statement, "I am alive." He specified where he was and what he had undergone. His agony had been "terrible" but he now had hopes "that I will live. This morning I had but little." He reported that Tom Norwood was with him at the Richeys' and had "fought a very hero's fight [at Second Manassas] firing twenty four rounds after receiving his painful wound standing the foremost . . . & never deserting his post." If Rufus or anyone else from Caldwell would decide to come and bring Tom and himself home, he explained that the best route to Middleburg was via Lynchburg and Gordonsville.

In the meantime, he would console himself with the only thoughts that had granted him a "spell of cheerfulness" during his suffering—his belief that if he were to die, it would be "in a most just & righteous cause." Without a hint of irony, he noted that he was writing on "a Yankee sheet of paper & envelope," supplies seized as the rebels drove the Yankees off the plains at Manassas Junction. In case Rufus was wondering about the stains on the paper, he explained that he had stuffed the stationery into a pocket "as I lay soaking in the heavy rain & my own blood on the battle field of Manassas." He closed by stressing that through all his tears "I send you all my love intensified as it never was before."

His first three weeks brought him limited relief. Although his appetite returned faster than expected, he was unable to sleep. Forced to remain slightly elevated on his back so that his throbbing stump could drain, he could not relax to the point of benefiting from a sound sleep. "The sleep famine," as he called it, was "horrible. The days were like months." Finally, his stump healed sufficiently to permit him to turn over on his side, and his exhausted body was able to find the rest it craved. During those endless days he thought constantly of his loved ones at home and was conscious of a "new spiritual strength." Ever since he had joined the army, and especially once he had known that he would command his own company in Virginia, he had tried to reach out to God and experience the rebirth that would signal his redemption. Surely that was all his mother had ever asked of him since he was old enough to go to college. Now, lying on his bed of agony, desperately needing to find meaning in his terrible wounds, he wrote to his mother that he viewed his suffering "as part of God's dealings with me as a sinner. And although his chastisements which I have brought upon myself have seemed very fierce, his mercies & his loving kindness which he has at the same time showereth upon me, have seemed more overwhelming still, though, all undeserved." The world that had turned his heart into stone never seemed farther from him nor God closer. "I loved to think of God and to pray to him and to read and hear his word." He could not read the Gospel of St. John to Tom Norwood and a fellow convalescing soldier without finding "new meaning" in the familiar words and breaking into tears. He had little doubt, he told his mother, that he would finally join the church when he returned home.

The new identity he would assume as a professed Christian, Walter was convinced, would complete the transformation in his character wrought by the war. This sense of newness, of shedding an old self for a new one, was by no means uncommon among Civil War soldiers. For many, the totality of the war experience made their civilian past seem like an odd relic of their imaginations. Certainly that was the case for Bolivar Christian, Nealy's brother. Like Walter, he had been a lawyer before the war who found no particular satisfaction in his profession. Also present at the Battle of Second Manassas, he wrote to Walter as soon as he learned of his wounds. In addition to urging Walter to borrow any money he might need and to use the family homestead to rest and to mend, he asked Walter if the war had changed him. "I…am unlike—I hope—what I ever was before in civil life," he confided. "In Winchester a lady acquaintance asking me so many questions to which I had to answer 'don't know'—finally asked me if I *knew myself*—I replied hadn't *seen* myself for 6 months. I suppose you were as *unlikely* as myself."

In Walter's case, the change was experienced as a softening of his heart, a new sensibility of suffering that embraced virtues he had identified with women before the war. The war had opened him up to the "finer feelings" of his nature. As an officer, he found himself in the motherly role of caring for and consoling his men. Their "hard fare, their weary gait, their bare and bleeding feet and parched lips, and their heroic patience" brought him to the point of tears. Hard campaigning effaced his former "life of comparative ease and indolence" and brought him face-to-face with suffering that formerly he had ignored. Even more powerful than this outpouring of concern for his men was the intensified tenderness for his family. "But it was not till the very marrow of my soul had been touched by my sufferings after I was wounded," he later wrote in his journal, "that my love for my mother and my brothers gushed forth as it had never done before. The slightest mention of any of their names every thought of them caused my tears to start, and my voice to falter and fail. My feelings of love for them had never been so intensified before; will probably never be again, unless it be when I am stretched upon my dying bed."

While this flood of emotions was reshaping Walter's sense of himself, his brother Rufus at Fort Defiance was struggling with emotions of a different sort. Although aroused by anger and not by love, these emotions also drew him closer to his mother. Rufus hated nothing more than disciplining a slave. It brought out the worst in him. This particular case involved Delia, a young slave woman who was continually "impudent" toward Selina, his widowed, seventy-eight-year-old mother. He would "thrash her," Rufus warned, if his mother ever complained of her behavior.

He spoke with Andy, Delia's father, in the hope that he could change her behavior, but to no avail. When Delia "gave Mother impudence again," Rufus ordered her into the house for a whipping. Crying out that "she could not stand that," she ran off to the kitchen, Rufus in pursuit. As he struggled to force her back into the house, Selina appeared and remarked that for all she cared Delia might as well be "dead." That was all the encouragement Rufus needed. Delia's only choice, he told her, was between a whipping in the house or a thrashing in the kitchen. "And after telling her three times that I would knock her down if she did not go, I gave her a tap which she will probably remember for some time."

Telling Tom of this confrontation, Rufus made it clear that it was time to be rid of the slaves who were troubling their aged and infirm mother. In addition to Delia, there was Maria, Andy's wife, "a very trifling hussy," who, "if she stays here will probably cause me to do something that will make me sorry afterward." Maria was Walter's slave, but he had told Rufus he should feel free to hire her out or pay someone to keep her if she ever troubled "his old mother." Given the unsettled affairs brought on by the war, and convinced that he would not be able to find any local takers for Maria, Rufus decided to ship her out to Haywood along with Andy and Delia. He suggested to Tom that they could be put to work on Walter's unrented Haywood land. Andy was "a first rate hand & a good servant," and Rufus knew that he would be more productive for Tom if he was not separated from his wife. He might have to send out two other slaves of Tom's as well, Polly and Beck, unless they showed more respect. Short of open defiance, he could put up with the slaves' sauciness, but it was different when his mother was involved. "I can stand a little of it myself but when mother complains I feel like hurting somebody."

Then Rufus learned of Walter's devastating wound and of his desire for Rufus to come and bring him home. Always the most rooted of the Lenoir brothers, Rufus was reluctant to leave. All his forebodings regarding the war returned and now he was being asked to abandon his wife and small children and trust that they would be protected in his absence. Still, Walter had virtually pleaded: "Dear Rufus please come to me at once." He could hardly refuse, but he put off the trip for two weeks and then discovered that the Confederate military was turning back civilians seeking to enter central Virginia via the most direct rail line. Rufus began a detour north and west through East Tennessee and southwestern Virginia to Alexandria. From there he would follow the Blue Ridge south and reach Middleburg by walking and riding. But Rufus encountered an outbreak of smallpox and turned back at Gordonsville. He ran into a member of Walter's company, who informed him that Walter was doing well and could be moved within a few weeks. Relieved both that his brother's life was not in immediate danger and that there was no pressing need for him to push on and confront Walter in his distressed condition, Rufus headed back to his family.

Unlike Rufus, Tom Lenoir moved quickly when he learned of Walter's fate. Tom reached Middleburg on September 23, a day after Yankee cavalry had passed through. He stayed with Walter until he was well enough to begin the journey home. They journeyed first to Richmond, where Walter checked into an army hospital and filled out the forms for his medical furlough. By mid-October he and Tom were back at Fort Defiance.

Walter returned home as a war hero. His niece Louise Norwood echoed the sentiments of family and friends when she spoke of his wound as "an *honor*" which "renders you dearer to us than ever, & we will always be proud of the gallant conduct which cost you so dear…You will not even be crippled," she added comfortingly, "for I am told that an artificial leg can be put on below the knee, which will 'act'…almost as well as the natural limb."

Walter's wound also provided him a safe conduct from the horrors of combat. Although (or perhaps because) he was now surrounded by women who wanted nothing more than to care for him and nurse him back to health, his thoughts drifted back to the battlefield and the bonds forged with the men serving under him. His reentry into civilian life threatened to undo that newfound sense of himself as a manly warrior enduring hardship and sacrifice for God and country. Initially, he thought he would never again desire a return to battle. But reports of the upcoming confrontation at Fredericksburg, Virginia, in December 1862, stirred up emotions. "Strange to say I…found myself growing restless at the thought that my old companions in arms were to be in another great battle, and I found myself actually longing to be with them in the fight."

In yearning to recapture the intoxicating sense of combat, to reexperience the most intense, passionate feelings he had ever known, Walter was of course fantasizing. He sent in his medical resignation from military service to take effect on December 18, and it was officially approved. God, as well as the peculiar ardor of combat, was also slipping away. Walter was unable to recapture that otherworldly sense of closeness to God that overwhelmed him as he lay helpless in Middleburg. As his health slowly returned at Fort Defiance, he lamented that "the vivid religious impressions which I felt during my period of great suffering seem to be giving way to too much of the coldness and apathy which have for, alas! so many years attended my religious course." His confession of faith would have to wait.

Of more immediate concern were Walter's fading hopes that his amputation could be easily overcome with a prosthetic device. His stump healed by mid-December, and he was able to hobble about on level ground with a clumsy wooden leg made by Rufus. But progress was slow. He first expressed his frustration in late December when he learned that his brother Tom was confined to bed after an ill-fated expedition into Tennessee. A month earlier, Tom and his North Carolina militia had been ordered to round up plundering bands of deserters and Tories (i.e., Unionists) in the mountains of East Tennessee. Tom thought they numbered anywhere from 800 to 2,000 and were "very bitter in their feelings toward the Southern men."

He had to be careful not to lead his men into an ambush. Earlier in the fall, three Confederates had gone into the mountains searching for what they had been told was a band of three Tories. The woman guiding them broke out in a song signaling their arrival to the waiting Tories. There were about ten of the enemy, not three, and they killed one of their pursuers and forced the others to flee for help.

Tom's cavalry unit aimlessly thrashed around East Tennessee for a week. Apart from killing one deserter and taking a couple dozen prisoners, the mission was a failure. Two nights without shelter in a drenching rain left Tom with a debilitating cold, and he returned home feverish and weak. When Walter heard of his condition, he felt helpless over his inability to assist his brother. Never before, he wrote Tom's wife Lizzie, had he so keenly felt the loss of his leg. Even if he could make it to Haywood, "I have so poor a use of myself," he wrote Lizzie, "that I would only be in the way if I were with you."

More disappointing news followed from Bolivar Christian, who had vainly searched for a manufacturer of wooden legs in Richmond. "I can hear of no foot or leg factory," he reported. "The demand as yet is but for crutches. The wounded being all too proud of their lameness to conceal it." Instead, Walter enlisted the services of a local carpenter, Samuel Montgomery. In late January, the two men examined the contrasting styles of wooden legs used by two amputees, a Mr. Wakefield and a Mr. Stockton. Palmer of Philadelphia manufactured the most commonly used wooden leg, one designed for amputees with a short stump. Stockton used this model, folding back his stump at the knee and resting it directly on the artificial limb. Wakefield, who had a longer stump that could not easily be folded back, opted for the model made by Ord of Philadelphia. His device had a ring into which he inserted his stump, so that it was supported at the point where his leg bones swelled below the joint of his knee. Without the ring, he never could have withstood the pain of folding over his long and tender stump and having it press down on a wooden leg. The major drawback was that the Ord required considerable time and effort to use with any degree of balance and confidence. Neither model impressed Walter. Yet he now knew that with a stump six inches long, the only option for "his Montgomery leg" was a ring attachment. He would "have to make up my mind to be a worse cripple than I had hoped for," he concluded.

While Montgomery worked on his leg, Walter forged ahead with his plans to move out to land he owned near Tom's farm in Haywood County, a mountainous and isolated region in the southwestern corner of the state. That course of action was the only way he knew to regain the manly independence he had come to value so highly as a Confederate soldier. To remain at home a cripple under the care of women only heightened the fears of emasculation he first sensed when visions of sexual inadequacy swirled through his mind as he lay helpless in the crossroads near Ox Hill. The shock and then anger expressed by his mother and sister upon hearing of his decision confirmed in his mind that he had to get away.

Walter followed Rufus's suggestion of sending Andy and his family out to Tom's farm in Haywood. In addition to providing Walter with his household labor, they would serve as the backbone of the labor force he needed for his own mountain farm. In urging Tom to put Andy to work as soon as possible, Walter praised his reliability and noted that Rufus had paid Andy $48 for the crops he produced in his family garden. Like many slave owners, the Lenoirs allowed their slaves to farm small plots of land set aside for their use and sell the produce to their masters. This was shrewd management, for the cash purchases reduced the temptation on the part of the slaves to engage in illicit trading with poor whites.

Walter also turned to his slave property to raise cash for his move and pay off debts. In February 1863 he sold Judy and her two youngest children, slaves he had inherited from his brother William's estate, for $1,700. He entered the slave market at a propitious time. Measured in Confederate currency, slave prices turned sharply upward beginning in the summer of 1862. Some of this increase reflected growing confidence in Confederate victory brought on by a string of military successes, but most of it tracked the accelerating depreciation of Confederate currency. The cheapening of the government's paper money inflated prices throughout the economy. Although many sellers wondered if the money they were receiving would soon be worth less than the slaves whose labor they were losing, the temptation to sell at high prices was often irresistible.

Rufus joined Walter in selling some of his estate slaves a few weeks after hearing from James Gwyn of the high slave prices in neighboring Wilkes County. Although Gwyn kicked himself for selling too soon back in January, he received what he characterized as "exorbitant" prices for two of his slaves. He was glad to be rid of both. Although he "disliked very much" separating Polly, a young slave girl, from her parents, he defended her sale by noting that "she got too far along in the slight of hand to keep." Lark, the other slave and a "No. 1 boy" in the classification scale of the slave trade, "had taken it into his head to engage in speculation & of course to succeed must travel about a good deal. I am opposed to that business generally & I thought he & I would not agree so well in the future & I sold him."

Walter intended to use some of the proceeds from his sales to reimburse Tom for money owed him from William's estate. By the winter of 1862–1863, however, the Southern backcountry was lapsing into a barter economy as more and more Confederates refused to accept their government's money. What Tom wanted from Walter wasn't depreciating money but goods like leather, cloth, and bolts of yarn that Tom could use to pay farm help reluctant to accept Confederate dollars. "I could sometimes get work for such articles," he explained, "when folks won't look at money."

Tom, like other Confederate civilians, was feeling the pinch of war-induced shortages in labor and consumer goods. Demand for iron goods from his blacksmith shop had never been greater, but he lacked the labor to meet it. He had half a mind to close the shop except on rainy days. Even before Yankee raiders swept down from East Tennessee in early January and burned the bridges to the nearest saltworks, he and Lizzie were making do with less than half of their normal supply of salt, which was essential for preserving meat. Only a favored few families in Haywood still had access to the cotton cards needed to prepare cotton for spinning in domestic manufacturing, and waits of up to six months for cotton to spin into clothing were now common.

Closer to transportation and textile factories, Caldwell County residents were able to meet most of their consumer needs. Still, it took Walter several weeks to stockpile the goods Tom and Lizzie had asked him to bring out to Haywood, and he had to settle for much less than they wanted. For Walter, these difficulties simply confirmed his belief that Southerners would have to sacrifice to gain their independence. Like most of his friends and associates, he believed in early 1863 that Confederate victory was only a matter of time. The successful defense of Richmond in the summer of 1862, followed by Confederate offensives into Maryland and Kentucky, the stabilization of the lines in the West, and the Union debacle at Fredericksburg, had bolstered morale on the home front and left many expecting an end to the war in 1863. Joe Norwood felt that "if the Yankees give us a chance, I think they will be badly whipped every where. And that will precipitate them into revolution or peace." Walter's cousin William Bingham boasted in March, "We are stronger than we have ever been since the war began. We make an abundant supply of arms & powder, have men enough, notwithstanding the Yankee conscription; and the Lord of Hosts is on our side." Although less strident, Walter was just as confident when he wrote Tom in February that "our cause is brighter and more hopeful than it has ever been before, but the greatest and fiercest battles of the war have still to be fought before the Yankees will be convinced."

For most of the remainder of the war, Walter waited for the Yankees to be convinced while he lived in a cramped cabin with his slaves in the mountain remoteness of Haywood County. In early April, he finally took delivery of his new Montgomery leg. By offering a hundred dollars, he was able to secure a hauler to bring his supplies out to Haywood. Walter went ahead on his horse Rip and three days later on April 17 reached Tom's place. He was brimming with hope. He proudly wrote home that he had "stood the journey so well as to feel gratified by it, and more in hopes that I may yet manage to be of some account."

Notes

For a full account of the battle in which Walter was severely wounded, see David A. Welker, *Tempest at Ox Hill: The Battle of Chantilly* (New York: Da Capo, 2002). Perhaps because the memory was so painful, Walter did not attempt to recall in writing what had happened to him at Ox Hill until he resumed his diary on January 10, 1863. He did not think he'd be able "to give as vivid an account of my feelings and impressions upon going into battle as I might have done immediately afterwards," and he was right. His account of his reaction to the battle at Cedar Mountain in a letter to Rufus on August 19, 1862, is more vivid and detailed than the recollection of the battle he included in his long diary entry of January 10 relating his experiences from late July to the moment he woke up from his leg amputation. The final entry a week later describes his harrowing wagon trip to Middleburg and the first months of his recuperation. Fittingly, the diary concludes with a note that effective December 18, 1862, he resigned from the army and "ceased to be a soldier."

The 37th North Carolina regiment lost fourteen men killed and ninety wounded in the fighting at Second Manassas and Ox Hill. Walter's Company A, which was especially hard hit, continued to see some of the heaviest fighting of the war. Twenty percent of the 206 men who served in the company throughout the war died of combat wounds, a rate of battlefield deaths nearly twice that of the average in Confederate armies. For a roster of the men who served in the company and a summary of their war service, see Louis H. Manarin and Weymouth T. Jordan Jr., *North Carolina Troops, 1861–1865: A Roster*, vol. 9, *Infantry* (Raleigh, N.C.: Division of Archives and History, 1983), pp. 471–85.

At least 50,000 wounded soldiers shared Walter's experience of having a limb amputated during the war. The conditions they faced in the often hastily constructed field hospitals are examined by Horace Herndon Cunningham in *Field Medical Services at the Battles of Manassas (Bull Run)* (Athens: University of Georgia Press, 1968). On the broader topic of Civil War medical care and knowledge, see Frank F. Freemon, *Gangrene and Glory: Medical Care during the American Civil War* (Madison, N.J.: Fairleigh Dickinson University Press, 1998); and Ira M. Rutkow, *Bleeding Blue and Gray: Civil War Surgery and the Evolution of American Medicine* (New York: Random House, 2005).

Ansley Herring Wegner, *Phantom Pain: North Carolina's Artificial-Limbs Program for Confederate Veterans, Including an Index to Records in the North Carolina State Archives Related to Artificial Limbs for Confederate Veterans* (Raleigh, N.C.: Office of Archives and History, 2004) includes a brief history of amputation and discusses the special problems confronting amputees. North Carolina's artificial limb program, the first of its kind in the South, offered amputees an artificial limb free of charge and a commutation fee of $70 to those who wished to purchase their own artificial leg. Wegner's index reveals that Walter submitted a request for the commutation fee on May 15, 1866.

· *Four* ·

MOUNTAIN FARMER

———

Walter fell in love with his mountain farm, which he came to see as "perhaps the prettiest place in all the wild mountains." Part of its appeal to him was its solitude, the sense of isolation he craved as he sought to prove to himself and others that his crippling wound had not robbed him of his manly independence.

Crab Orchard, as Walter called his farm, was a few miles above Tom and Lizzie's place on the East Fork of the Pigeon River. He set up house in a drafty, windowless, one-room cabin infested with vermin. Trying to make it habitable, he spent the first two weeks daubing cracks in the siding, setting the floor of the cabin closer to the ground, and making a bedstead so he would not have to sleep on the floor. His nine slaves were packed into an even smaller cabin, which also served as a kitchen. The outbuildings consisted of a dilapidated corncrib and a chicken coop that Walter converted into a smokehouse. No lots had been fenced for livestock and the ditching and fencing were badly in need of repair.

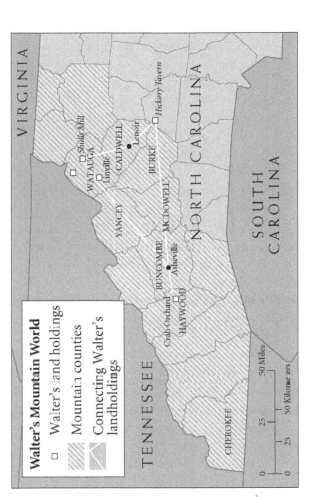

Walter's mountain world.

After his move to Haywood, Walter rarely left the North Carolina mountains. From his homes at Crab Orchard and then Shulls Mill, he traveled extensively visiting the large landholdings he acquired after the war.

While he was supervising his slaves' work on the furniture for his simple cabin, Walter could spend evenings thinking about how the war had brought him to where he was now. In the months and years ahead, he would spend much time thinking about why he had fought—why they all had—and whether the sacrifice would prove worth it. Although he never put it so starkly, he was deciding on the history he needed to understand his world after the war. As he tried to square his present world with the one he had known before the war, it would have been hard for him to avoid a sense of self-righteousness—a sort of sanctimonious smugness—in knowing that he had faced up to and survived the carnage on the battlefields. As a result, he was incapable of imagining that his sacrifices and those of other Confederates had been in vain. The more he thought, the holier the war became, and he was incapable—indeed refused—to remember what had caused the war and the hideous side of how it was fought. In short, his survivor's memory of the war was a self-biased one. But for now, his thoughts returned to his farm and all the dreams he had invested in it.

Even with two good legs, Walter would have faced a challenge in turning the site into a flourishing stock farm. As it was, he was utterly dependent on his slaves. "I will do a little if my negroes prove industrious and honest," he wrote Rufus. "If they turn out badly, I may find myself going down hill so fast that I will have to give up them and my land and put myself out to board with somebody, but I will not write myself a cypher till I find that I am."

Only three of Walter's slaves—Uriah and Andy and his wife Maria—were adults. On them rested the entire burden of feeding Walter, putting in and tending his crops, and caring for the livestock. No white hands were available as day laborers. The draft had taken off the adult men who had not volunteered, and Walter's tenants were by now mostly women and children who unavoidably were falling behind in their rental payments of corn.

This was the wooden leg Walter favored.
(SOURCE: *North Carolina Collection, Wilson Library, University of North Carolina–Chapel Hill.*)

Tom tried to help out with provisions of bacon, but there was a limit to what he could set aside for Walter and destitute families once Confederate officers began scouring the mountains seizing supplies for the army in a policy known as impressment.

While Walter was slowly and painfully learning how to get around on his Montgomery leg, he entrusted everything to Andy and Maria, including his only lock, one used for the corncrib. Andy did the plowing for the first crop of corn, oats, and Irish potatoes (common white potatoes as opposed to the typical Southern crop of sweet potatoes). Maria was in charge of the meat and a flock of chickens that kept Walter supplied with eggs. Turnip greens from the slaves' garden patch, along with milk from their cow, were welcome additions to the cornbread and bacon diet. When not needed by Tom, Uriah helped out with the farm chores. On the rare nights that Walter spent down at Tom and Lizzie's, Uriah stayed in Walter's cabin, guarding it against neighbors noted for their stealing. Walter's main contribution to the farm consisted of planting some grafts of apple, plum, and pear stocks. The one day he spent in the fields helping Andy plant the corn left his stump so sore that he was nearly ready to give up using his Montgomery leg.

Measured by his tax assessment, Uriah was Walter's most valuable slave and, along with Andy, he was indispensable to any plan for improvements. Not wanting to alienate such a valuable slave, Walter grudgingly consented to Uriah's marriage to Delia, one of Tom's slaves whom Walter considered "of little account." The marriage was part of a double ceremony for two slave couples held on the night of May 16 at the Den, Tom's name for his Haywood home. Lewis Welsh, a black preacher, performed the ceremony. In

Walter's mocking words, the preacher had been "duly authorized by the law (Ethiopian) to celebrate the bans of matrimony, and also to hear and determine actions of debt and pleas of assault and battery and other breaches of the peace [among the slaves] and to pronounce judgment and issue execution." Although Walter dismissed as pretentious the preacher's claim to wield real authority, the slaves acknowledged his power and relied on his rulings to settle disputes among themselves. In helping maintain the slaves' morale and thereby their productivity, the preacher was ultimately Walter's ally.

With the exception of an occasional newspaper from Asheville, Walter relied on letters from relatives in Caldwell and from his nephew Tom Norwood in Virginia for information on the war outside of the mountains of North Carolina. Most of the news in the spring of 1863 was discouraging. Norwood, who was ordered back to the North Carolina 37th in the spring after his foot had healed, reported that "our company has disgraced itself by descrtion," six men while Tom was home recuperating, and another thirty soon after Norwood's return, including four who had served under Walter. Tom Lenoir was kept busy that spring leading scouting parties in a fruitless attempt to round up the Haywood deserters. Back in Caldwell, Rufus was convinced that his enemies on the tax assessing board had overvalued his property in hopes of forcing him to pay more than his fair share in war taxes. Brother-in-law James Gwyn had also quarreled with a prominent Unionist over the issue of accepting Confederate paper money in payment of prewar debts. When the Unionist taunted the secessionist Gwyn with the argument that he ought to take the money of the government that he and the other secessionists had clamored for, Gwyn

Increasing numbers of deserters hid out in the mountains of North Carolina.
(Source: *Courtesy of the North Carolina State Archives.*)

replied that he'd be damned if he would accept currency worth only a quarter of the money he had loaned out in 1858.

As spring turned into summer and casualty lists spiked upward, the first signs of an inner civil war appeared in the mountain counties. Most of the troops raised in these counties served in Lee's army. After suffering high casualties in the Seven Days Battles, they incurred even heavier losses at Gettysburg in July 1863. The one bright spot was news that Tom Norwood, listed as missing for over a week, not only survived the battle but emerged as a war hero. Taken prisoner after being wounded thirty yards from the Union batteries, Tom escaped from a building at Gettysburg College, made his way through Federal pickets, fell in with Confederate sympathizers, and eventually enjoyed a breakfast with General Lee at which he passed on valuable information about the Union lines he had circled around as he escaped. Tom's cousin and a female friend were so excited on hearing of Tom's escape that they "had a mind to retreat to the woods and just holler our very ravingest until our emotions subsided."

Tom's story brought joy to the Norwoods, but most mountain families received the news from Gettysburg with growing despair. The men they had sent off to the army were overwhelmingly non-slaveholders whose labor was essential to their mountain farms. Their absence left more and more families impoverished and desperately hungry. As the war dragged into its third year, despair turned into open resistance to Confederate authorities and their hated draft and impressment policies. From the ranks of these mountain farmers came most of the deserters and the outliers, men trying to avoid the draft by fleeing from their homes and lying out the war. Numbering between 200 and 300, they roamed Caldwell County in the summer of 1863 pillaging for supplies, especially from prominent secessionist families. Larger bands swept through neighboring Wilkes and Yadkin counties.

Linking up with diehard Unionists, the deserter bands were most defiant in the small community of Trap Hill in northern Wilkes, not far from the Green Hill plantation of James and Mary Ann Gwyn in Ronda. They shocked local Confederates by organizing a Union militia and raising a U.S. flag—that "old dirty United States rag," as Mary Ann's daughter, Julia, put it. After dismissing the Unionists as "poor fools" acting out of "ignorance," Mary Ann admitted that "our neighbors here have nearly all *deserted* who were in the army—some who fought bravely too!" In the spring of 1861

Southern women had urged their men to do their duty and return as heroes from the war. Now, Julia reported, "the women write to their husbands to leave the army and come home and that's the reason so many of them are deserting." She added with disgust that "some of the people about here are actually rejoiced at the death of Genl. Jackson! … I wish the Yankees had the last one of them."

Stonewall Jackson, accidentally wounded by his own troops soon after spearheading a stunning Confederate victory at Chancellorsville, Virginia, had died on May 10 from an infection that set in after his left arm was amputated. His loss was the first in a series of blows sustained by the Confederacy in the spring and summer of 1863. Lee's defeat at Gettysburg resulted in 28,000 casualties, a staggering one-third of his effective force. A day later, on July 4, the Confederacy lost Vicksburg, its main fortress on the Mississippi River, and surrendered its defending army of 30,000 men. Four days later, the secondary river fortress of Port Hudson, Louisiana, fell. Before the month was out, the Union gained control of middle Tennessee, one of the prime sources of food for Confederate armies. On the home front many questioned whether the Confederacy would ever be able to mobilize all of its resources to support its armies. "In the meantime," a despondent Joe Norwood wrote Walter, "desertion is rife, the men regard their money as worthless & the government is unable to remedy the evil."

Through this summer of discontent, Walter's faith remained that of a zealot who had converted to a new religion. He reduced the war to a struggle between absolute good and evil and spoke increasingly of the war in religious terms. Lee was not just a skilled general, but "a noble hearted Christian soldier." Walter expressed "love and admiration" for Southern soldiers, convinced that Lee's soldiers had, with a few regrettable but understandable exceptions, treated the people of Pennsylvania with kindness and restraint. Their behavior would "shine out forever in bright contrast with the infamous conduct of our enemies."

While he did not dismiss the recent Confederate setbacks, he insisted that these defeats were more symbolic than substantive. It was remarkable, he wrote Joe Norwood, that Vicksburg had held out so long. To be sure, the Yankees now controlled the Mississippi and were in a position to isolate the trans-Mississippi West; yet the West "was already virtually isolated" before Vicksburg fell. The worst that could happen now would be more Yankee raids east of the river. "The war will move on, pretty much as it has done," he assured Norwood, "and we will finally discomfit them."

Rufus was less sure, especially after Lincoln announced that his Emancipation Proclamation would go into effect on January 1, 1863. In a move designed to break the two-year military stalemate, Lincoln called for the freeing of all slaves in areas still under Confederate control as of the beginning of 1863 and announced that the Union would accept freed slaves in military service. Walter knew well that Rufus's darkest forebodings centered on a war that unleashed scenes of "assassination and general massacre" in which the slaves would rise up to exact revenge from their masters. He wrote Rufus a long letter in late July attempting to soothe his fears that Lincoln's proclamation was a call for a bloody slave insurrection.

The Yankees had been freeing slaves since the start of the war, he reassured Rufus. In practical terms their conduct now was simply a continuation of earlier policy. More disturbing was the Union's enlistment of black troops beginning in the spring of 1863. Initially, Walter had thought that the number of black troops would be small, just enough "to keep the South in a state of excitement." After all, white Union soldiers would hardly wish to serve with them. Besides, like most Southern whites, and many Northerners as well, he could never envision blacks developing into competent soldiers. He imagined that they would run under the pressure of battle and, once captured, would be executed along with their white officers as criminals guilty of inciting a slave insurrection. He clearly had been mistaken. The Union was raising more black troops than he expected, Confederates were taking them as prisoners of war, not shooting them on the spot when captured, and, as he conceded to Rufus, "it is so natural to man to fight that it is possible that even the negro disciplined and led by white men may stand fire better than we of the South have supposed." Nonetheless, he continued to believe that the Yankees would sharply limit the combat use of its black troops.

As for emancipation, Walter had at first ruled out any possibility because he could not bring himself to believe that an all-merciful God would allow the Yankees "to perpetrate so great a crime as that against us and their species." Forced emancipation, he assumed, would result in "horrid massacre and butchery" as enraged slaves, their passions inflamed by the abolitionists, rose up to slay whites. Acting out of self-defense, the whites would be compelled to slaughter their former slaves in the ensuing race war. Such a nightmarish vision had been a staple of Southern thought since the massive and violent slave revolt on the Caribbean island of St. Domingue in the 1790s. Of course, as Walter acknowledged, mere mortals could hardly fathom the workings of divine will. By the summer of 1863, the Yankees were indeed freeing significant numbers of slaves, forcing Walter to consider whether God's will might be that "our enemies may succeed in this." If so, they would do so "without any massacres except such as are now taking place on the battle field … Bad as the Yankees are they would not wish the whites of the South to be massacred by the negroes and would not permit it."

In support of this extraordinary shift in his thinking, Walter reminded Rufus that Yankee emancipation in southern Louisiana had proceeded peacefully after the Confederacy lost New Orleans in the spring of 1862. The orderly transition had occurred even with Louisiana's high concentration of slaves ruled by sugar planters notorious for treating their slaves harshly. Surely, Walter argued, if these slaves had not retaliated against whites in an orgy of violence, there was little chance of it happening elsewhere in the South.

Jamaica provided another hopeful example in the Caribbean. In marked contrast to St. Domingue, emancipation in Jamaica and the other British sugar islands in the 1830s was an orderly process that preserved the plantation economy. To be sure, Jamaica's sugar output declined as freed slaves abandoned the plantations to become a poor peasantry, and the South might suffer a similar fate, Walter conceded, if it lost the war. But there would be no horrific scenes of black vengeance against whites. "If the Yankees are strong enough to put down our fierce and strong fight of independence," Walter concluded, "they will be strong enough to govern the negroes afterwards."

Walter assured Rufus that he thought the Union effort would bog down once its armies tried to penetrate into the Confederate interior. Its major victories in taking New Orleans, Memphis,

THE MAKING OF A CONFEDERATE

Vicksburg, and Port Hudson resulted from its unmatched naval superiority. But sooner or later the Union would have to turn its campaigns inward away from the coast and rivers, and then Confederate armies would turn the invaders back with heavy losses. Pointing to the growing strength of a Northern peace party, Walter was confident that Confederate resistance would cost Lincoln his reelection bid in 1864 and force him "to hand over the job unfinished to his successor." With a Democrat in the presidency, the Confederacy could expect recognition of its independence.

For all his confidence, Walter could not ignore the mounting evidence of unrest on the home front. In August he heard from Joe Norwood of "a terrible state of things upon the Tennessee line, particularly in Watauga." Roving bands of bushwhackers were pillaging at will, and one of their raids resulted in the death of Thomas Farthing, a friend of the Lenoirs' and a well-known secessionist. Tom Norwood, home on medical leave recuperating from his wound at Gettysburg, was sent out to Ashe, another mountain county, to bring back thirty-one deserters from his company.

What most concerned Walter was the rising public demand to end the war, a demand that did not always insist on Southern independence as a precondition for peace. Leading the call for a negotiated end to the war was William W. Holden, the maverick editor of the Raleigh *North Carolina Standard*. A reluctant secessionist and a lukewarm Confederate early in the war, Holden emerged in the summer of 1863 as North Carolina's most prominent critic of the Confederate government. His editorials charged Richmond with erecting a military despotism that was trampling the Southern liberties it was formed to uphold. Especially after the terrible casualties suffered by North Carolina regiments at Gettysburg, Holden's call for a speedy peace served as a rallying call for disenchanted Confederates. Peace meetings were held across the state in the summer of 1863, nine of them in the mountain counties close to Haywood.

Worried that Rufus was on the verge of becoming a craven submissionist willing to forfeit his rights in a Yankee-dictated peace, Walter redoubled his efforts to shore up his brother's faltering patriotism. In the late summer and fall he accused Rufus of all but wishing for further Confederate defeats, an attitude he called "sinful." Rufus's complaints over the lack of salt for preserving meat were curtly dismissed with the observation that "meat is a luxury. The Roman soldiers who conquered the world [ate] little or no flesh." Hoping to shame Rufus out of being "so incorrigibly blue," he asked, "Who that deserves to be free would not rather wander forty years in the wilderness and live on bread alone rather than return to the flesh pots and be a slave?" Their French Huguenot ancestors, after being driven out of their country for their religious beliefs, had sired a "long race of Lenoirs" who prospered in the South as the "best farmers" who got the "best lands and the best wives." Rufus should face the future with the same resolution they had shown. God nurtured his chosen people with tribulations; he laid "the heaviest afflictions on those who have most need of his love and favor."

"Cheer up then," he concluded. "Look the worst squarely in the face if you will, and still be a man." Walter stressed that Rufus owed nothing less to himself, his family, and the Confederate soldiers who were valiantly defending Southern freedoms.

If the unthinkable happened and the Confederacy were defeated, Walter had made up his mind to leave the South and live in exile before subjecting himself to the "hell on earth that the South would become." When the fall of Vicksburg on July 4, 1863, led many to openly talk of what terms the South might be able to get from the North, he reflected on the course "it might be my duty to take." If he still "had two legs," he would have been fighting as a soldier and his choice would have been made for him. "But I was no longer able to give battle, I could not even promise myself the poor consolation which I intended to have of killing the first Yankee or traitor who should come into possession of my dwelling." After three days meditating on his proper duty, his spirits lifted with the realization that "I had but to bring the proposition before my mind to be convinced that I could never submit to Yankee rule."

What made the thought of remaining in the defeated South intolerable to Walter was his assumption that the racial and class privileges he and his family had enjoyed as members of North Carolina's white elite would be swept aside in a radically transformed social order. Despite all the evidence to the contrary, he understood peace advocates who talked of trying to reconstruct the old Union not as loyal Southerners who had grown weary of the war and its sacrifices but as covert abolitionist sympathizers who lusted after the planters' lands and female slaves. "I believe that every reconstructionist is an abolitionist at heart, and likes Lincoln's emancipation proclamation," he wrote Rufus. "I would suspect on very slight grounds that he was an amalgamationist and had some notion of taking a negro wife." The thought of living to see the power relations of his prewar world turned upside down filled him with a visceral hatred. Rather than "become the fellow citizen" of poor whites, "liable to be elbowed out of the road by them or to see my mother or my sisters insulted by the wenches who would flank the highway with them, I would rather lose all my property, loathe in a dungeon, die." He might be "too poor and weak and helpless to get away," but the goal of escaping from such a hellhole along with the "best people of the South" would give him something to live for after the collapse of the Confederacy.

Part of Walter seems to have welcomed the prospect of martyrdom in a life of exile. He was happier in his "lonely life" than he ever could have anticipated. His mountain farm grew "more and more beautiful to my eyes every day." But earthly happiness turned poor sinners away from their spiritual duties, he recognized. Despite the pleadings of his mother, he had not joined a church, a failure for which he had "no excuse but sin." "It may well be," he concluded, "that it would prove a great blessing for me to have to give up this life of comparative ease and enjoyment in this delightful place and enter upon a life of hard work and discomfort in some distant region, where I would feel like a mere sojourner." If affliction was good for the soul, Walter was ready to embrace it.

In the fall of 1863 Walter grew more optimistic over the Confederacy's prospects. A show of military force in September quelled the worst of the disturbances in the disaffected regions of central and western North Carolina. Governor Zebulon Vance, who had left the army in the summer of 1862 to run for the governorship, pleaded with the War Department for a regiment of Confederate troops once it was clear that the Home Guard, older men and teenagers ineligible for the draft, was incapable of restoring order. Richmond dispatched troops under General Robert F. Hoke, a native North Carolinian, to intimidate supporters of the peace movement and capture deserters and conscripts. Hoke rounded up 3,000 men, he claimed, but his rough methods did damage too. He forced deserters out of their hiding places by holding their farm property as ransom until the men turned themselves in. Meanwhile, Hoke's troops helped themselves to whatever they could carry off and destroyed the crops of those accused of sheltering deserters. Even a Confederate as loyal as James Gwyn felt that Hoke's men had gone too far and would "ruin the most of the people" who defied the Confederacy; "their crops were very poor anyway I understand & what they will make will be destroyed." The hard times they faced come winter and spring would worsen the very conditions that had fueled discontent in the first place.

While Hoke was punishing the dissidents in North Carolina, Tom Norwood rounded up over fifteen deserters from his company. The deserters were contrite after being brought back to Virginia and witnessing the stepped-up pace of executions for desertion in Lee's army. "I think the execution system is producing a fine effect on the men generally," Tom commented. He felt sure now that the Union army would never be able "to conquer us in the field."

News of the Confederate victory in September at Chickamauga in northern Georgia heartened Walter. He was cheered, too, by the increasingly defiant opposition to Lincoln's government led by the Peace Democrats, or the Copperheads as the Republicans called them. Most promising, he heard talk of powerful, blockade-busting rams that were being built in England for the

Confederacy. Those ships, he predicted, "will open the blockade on sight and turn the besiegers of our coasts into the besieged." Unknown to Walter, the British Foreign Office had given in to Union demands and detained the rams in England.

By early November Walter was boldly proclaiming to Joe Norwood that "our military situation, apart from the currency, is as hopeful as it ever has been." But the Confederate paper dollar had lost 90 percent of its purchasing power as measured in gold. Walter could only wish that early on the Confederate Congress had levied a tax on land and slaves, which comprised in value two-thirds of all the property in the Confederacy. The slaveholding elite who dominated the Congress had not wanted to tax their own property to pay for the war. Prodded by President Davis, Congress passed a direct tax on land and slaves in February 1864, but it was riddled with exemptions and valued land and slaves at their preinflated prices of 1860. The tax fell far short of raising the revenue needed to bolster the value of the currency.

Walter's hopes were clearly more wishful than realistic. The Confederate military effort in the fall of 1863 was at best buying time while the Union continued to draw on seemingly limitless resources of men and matériel. Despite intimations that they would recognize the Confederacy, the British held back from openly antagonizing the Union government. The successful Union campaigns in the summer of 1863 stiffened Northern resolve, and the Republicans won important fall elections in Ohio and Pennsylvania. After the elections Tom Norwood advised Walter to give up any hope that the Northern public would tire of trying to subjugate the South. Most significantly, Braxton Bragg failed to follow through on his victory at Chickamauga, allowing a Union army seemingly trapped in Chattanooga to turn the tables on him in November, rout his army, and send it retreating into northern Georgia.

Joe Norwood had every reason to feel "very much depressed about our national affairs" when he wrote Walter on November 17. Walter's cousins in East Tennessee had borne the full brunt of Union raids after the Yankees occupied Knoxville and much of the surrounding region. The Lenoirs there "suffered severely, it being understood through the country that all of the name were good friends to the Confederate States or as the Yanks call us secessionists." The next targets "to be overrun," Norwood feared, were the prominent Confederates in Caldwell and neighboring mountain counties.

Haywood was in easiest reach of Union raiders. In reporting to his sister Sarah on the "feeling of insecurity" that hung over Haywood, Walter noted that the Yankees "do their work of plunder pretty thoroughly now-a-days, sometimes not even leaving a change of clothes for the little girls." Gone was the optimism he had exuded a month earlier, replaced by the fear "that a more desperate struggle than ever is still before us, and the peace that must some day end it seems more distant than ever." Regardless of how the war turned out, he was pretty certain he would not be seeing additional service as a military judge. Back in the summer, his friends in the army and in the Vance administration had secured a judgeship for him in the Virginia military courts, but his maimed condition made it difficult for him to move around with the army hearing cases. Although he never admitted it directly, he had too much pride to run the risk of being pitied by his fellow officers.

The woolen clothes Sarah made for Walter and sent to Haywood helped him get through his first winter in the mountains. He had anticipated the cold weather but not the killing frost in September that cut into his harvest. Supplies of food were tight throughout the winter, especially after Confederates hunting for deserters and stray cattle lodged with him on several nights in February and helped themselves to his small stockpile of corn and bacon. Tom and Lizzie shared what little they had, and Walter looked the other way when his slaves supplemented their meager rations with food they bartered for in illicit trade with local whites. Still, the situation would have been critical had Yankee raiders swept through Haywood. Walter attributed their absence to the poor roads and poverty in the region.

As hard as the winter was, Walter's slaves enjoyed more comfortable living quarters in a new and larger cabin. The prohibitive cost of hauling cut lumber into the mountains had forestalled making improvements until he had a sawmill up and running in the fall. His slaves had worked hard enough to produce what would have been a decent harvest before the September frost, and they had tended the hogs well enough to put away 1,400 pounds of pork for the winter. Even so, Walter was convinced that they were shirking, especially the women. "Though I always considered she negroes a pest," he complained to his mother, "mine are dirtier and lazier than even I counted on." Blinded by his disdain, he simply could not understand why Maria, who was suffering from poor health after the birth of her last child in December, wanted to avoid work in the fields and had fallen behind in her spinning for the slaves' winter clothing. Having lacked the nerve to undertake "the very disagreeable task of instituting and keeping up a strict discipline," he blamed himself for his slaves' lackadaisical attitude. He had put off this "hard piece of work" half hoping that the Yankees would be "kind enough to take them off my hands." But if the Yankees stayed away, he vowed, his slaves would have "to make a great change soon, or have another master."

Apart from his brief and uncomfortable experience with Cyrus back in 1858, Walter had avoided the responsibility of managing slaves. For standards on provisions and labor demands for his slaves at Crab Orchard, he relied on detailed guidelines furnished by his mother. In March his sister Laura advised that it was "not worthwhile to expect much from negroes in a moral point of view, or in any other point of view. I think we ought to do what we reasonably can to make them do right, and not worry our lives out because we succeed very imperfectly." Walter conceded that he probably had set his standards too high. He had begun farming at Crab Orchard with the hope that his "system" for managing slaves "could make them a great deal better," but he now realized that his plans were "impracticable" and likely would result in "pecuniary sacrifice rather than profit." However, he urged Laura not to be concerned by his frustration; the ties that bound him to owning slaves were "so slight that my slaves *can't* habitually trouble me much." He was prepared at any time to be rid of them and was only awaiting "the dreary progress of this war before knowing how to decide these things."

Unfortunately for Rufus Lenoir that "dreary progress" had resulted in an encampment of Georgia troops on his land. General James Longstreet's troops were impressing supplies for an expected campaign in the spring of 1864 to push the Federals out of East Tennessee. Since early in the war the Confederate army had been seizing private property for government use whenever farmers were reluctant to sell goods whose price was constantly rising due to inflation. Longstreet's men seized 100 bushels of Rufus's corn, 100 pounds of bacon, and several wagonloads of hay. At night they simply took what they wanted—chickens, garden vegetables, and the seed potatoes needed for the next year's crop. Sarah felt that the officers treated the family with proper respect, but she was appalled by the behavior of their men, especially after "two of them were found making themselves comfortable and agreeable in our negro cabins." Supplies of corn were already low; now she worried whether there would be enough left to distribute to the poor. The situation would become even more dire if, as reported, Longstreet impressed all the horses and mules before he departed. "I tell you it is getting to be a reality that we are in danger of having what we have taken," reported Sarah, "and no chance to make half a crop next year." Rufus was spitting up blood from a lung condition, but at least that ensured he would not be drafted into the army.

In the end, President Davis ordered Longstreet back to Virginia on April 7 to reinforce Lee's army to meet the Union's spring offensive. Rufus had fared better than Sarah feared. Although impressment agents had taken his oxen, nine horses, and a mule, he was left with most of the farm animals he needed to put in his crops. Still, Walter's mother was relieved to see the troops go. They were a law unto themselves, she wrote Walter, "who pressed corn, bacon, horses, &c &c, without proper authority, and stole and cut up considerably."

The most heartening news Walter received in the spring of 1864 came from his nephew Tom Norwood. Stationed on the front lines of Lee's army waiting for Grant's long anticipated offensive, Tom assured Walter that "Grant will be whipped. Set that down." The spirit of the army had never been higher. Even the men in Walter's old Company A had reenlisted "with a zest" so that they could "blot out the big black mark against them (for desertion)." That "zest" may have been encouraged by the execution of two men for desertion only two weeks earlier. Privates George Black and Jeremiah Blackburn, the two men executed on April 14, were repeat offenders. The fact that each was married with a family gained them no leniency from the court-martial board. Blackburn had not even been seeing combat duty. After he shot off a finger in the summer of 1863 to avoid duty, he was detailed to serve at a Richmond hospital. He might have succeeded in sitting out the war had he not forged furlough papers for the absurdly long period of "1000 days."

From May 4 through late June, Grant's offensive pounded Lee's army almost daily, and the fighting spirit in Tom's regiment cooled considerably. Many in the 37th Regiment were now supporting William W. Holden for governor in the August election. Appealing to all who had supported the peace movement in 1863, Holden called for a state convention to open separate peace negotiations with the North. Walter had denounced Holden's plan as a "wild absurd blind delusion" in a letter to Governor Vance in April urging him to wage an all-out campaign against Holden, his opponent. Most North Carolina soldiers were even harsher in their assessment, attacking Holden as a traitorous defeatist who should be hanged for encouraging brave men to desert their posts of duty. The men of the 37th were a decided exception in their favorable view of Holden, hailing as they did from the western mountain counties, what Tom called "a sort of cool country." In his opinion they were never "very hot-blooded southerners any way." Their position, as he outlined it to Walter, was, "We admit the necessity of fighting now while they invade our country; but we were cheated into it at the start; had no primary interest in it, never to the latest generations expected to be benefited by it."

As Tom predicted, the men in the 37th cast a majority of their ballots for Holden. However, Vance swept to victory with 88 percent of the soldiers' vote and 77 percent of the civilian vote. As popular as Vance undoubtedly was, a heavy dose of intimidation against Holden's supporters, especially in the army, padded his huge majorities.

For Walter, as well as Tom Norwood and others in the shrinking but fanatical core of Confederate diehards, every loss of a friend or relative deepened the need to see the war through. In responding to the combat deaths of his cousins Mouton and William Waightstill Avery, Tom declared that "every day of my life I feel my love for our pure banner of Southern independence grow stronger & stronger, and my detestation of everything Yankee more & more intense. Oh it isn't hatred, it's *abhorrence*! Self defense urges us on to indefinite resistance & our wrongs cry for eternal *vengeance*!" Walter reacted with a similar fury when he heard that James Reagan, a Tennessee relative, had died in Yankee captivity in East Tennessee. Reagan's death, Walter wrote Rufus, was "willful murder," additional evidence that the Yankees offered Southerners only "subjugation or extermination."

The death Walter felt most deeply was his mother's. She died at Fort Defiance on September 23, 1864, never having seen Walter again after he left for Crab Orchard in the spring of 1862. As Walter knew only too well, she had viewed his departure as an abandonment of the family. She implored him to return repeatedly, and the longer he stayed away the more reproachful she became. Four months before her death, she bluntly asked him in a letter, "Was such a mind as yours bestowed to live the life of a Hermit? And will not its long continuance be detrimental in some ways, producing indifference, even selfishness[?]" Aside from trying to assure his mother that he would return for a visit as soon as he felt he could, Walter ignored her pleas. Selina's tone was often hurtful because she sensed what Walter never openly acknowledged: his newfound identity as a Confederate had eclipsed his ties to his family. To have stayed with his mother in his boyhood home in his crippled condition would have been a devastating blow to the independence he had so proudly forged as a Confederate soldier. Faced with dependency on his slaves at Crab Orchard or on his mother and sister at Fort Defiance, he chose a solitary life with his slaves.

Having vowed never to submit to Yankee rule, Walter could hardly allow himself to feel that his slaves ruled him. In November he reached a crisis. It probably was more than coincidental that his anger focused on Delia, the same young slave whose saucy back talk to their mother had so enraged Rufus two years earlier. For weeks she had been "uncontrollably sulky and sullen," he told his sister Sarah, "and to have submitted to [her conduct] would have been in effect to have resigned my position as head of the family, and have reduced myself to a plaything in the hands of my slaves." He avoided such humiliation by severely whipping Delia. He could not risk alienating the hard-working Uriah, Delia's husband, by selling off Delia, and he could not sell them as a couple since Uriah was owned by his brother William's estate. He resolved the problem by hiring them out to a neighbor. Before they left, he called on his brother Tom's assistance when he "whipped Delia till she humbled herself a little, which was not till she was well punished, for she tried very hard to 'stout it out.'" Echoing the language Tom used when he had had a similar experience with a slave, he concluded, "I did my duty; I can see it in no other light; and the effect on my other negroes seems so far and will I have no doubt continue to be very good." The effect was also doubtless "good" for Walter once he had projected onto the unfortunate Delia the anger he felt toward himself for abandoning his mother as she lay on her deathbed.

Of course, the Yankees could not be humbled so easily. The major Union offensives surged forward in the late summer and fall and ensured that Lincoln would easily be reelected in November. While Lee's dwindling army was immobilized in the trenches of Petersburg, the Confederacy lost Atlanta on September 1, and two months later William Tecumseh Sherman began the march that carried his unstoppable army into North Carolina by March 1865. Closer to home for the Lenoirs, Union cavalry rode out of secure bases in East Tennessee and harassed western North Carolinians in a series of major raids. Outlaw Unionists and mountain outliers compounded the misery as they pillaged at will.

As the boundary between the battlefield and home front broke down, the war for civilians became a matter of defending home and property. "The robbers & bushwhackers in Wilkes & Caldwell are becoming more insolent & aggressive," an alarmed

Rufus reported to Walter in early November. "We never go to bed without thinking they may come before morning." A week later, James Gwyn up in Wilkes County was also afraid to go to bed at night, "for they are committing robberies on some nearly every night & we are expecting them upon us constantly." The home guards were no match for the marauding bands, and regular Confederate troops could not be spared.

Anxiously, Rufus sounded out Walter on moving all but his essential farm stock out to Haywood. He would even be willing to dispense with the hogs that provided the slaves with most of their meat rations. Led by Erwin, the same slave who had given Tom so much trouble when he had taken over his father's plantation in Haywood, Rufus's slaves had been "very dishonest" and increasingly open in their pilfering from the plantation. If the war brought an end to slavery, Rufus would be glad to see his slaves go.

Walter replied that he had all the farm animals he needed and advised Rufus to sell off his livestock at the highest price he could get. What he left unsaid was that conditions in Haywood were no better than in Caldwell. Tom had just lost five sides of leather to thieves, and armed robbers were hitting homes all along the East Fork of the Pigeon. Walter tried to console himself by taking in the delights of his wilderness that he loved so deeply. "We have charming weather," he wrote Rufus in December. "This is a soft lovely moonlight night, as pleasant to stroll in as if it were June, and peace were made, and I had two legs, and some one here to love. The moon is as bright and the clouds as flitting and fantastic, as if the fierce conflicts and evil passions of this mighty war were only a merry revel or gay maskerade. The mood and clouds cannot think; but they seem to think it is all vanity."

By early 1865, the Confederate war effort might as well have been called a masquerade, one that could no longer conceal the impending collapse of the Confederacy. By March Union troops were occupying Wilmington, North Carolina, the last major port still open to blockade runners. A mounted regiment led by George Kirk, a Tennessee Unionist, terrorized mountain residents as it laid waste to farms and property in Haywood County, just bypassing the homes of Tom and Walter. On March 7, Sherman's fearsome army entered the state and headed toward Fayetteville.

As Union forces struck at will, political divisions deepened among the state's leaders. A peace-at-any-price faction in the legislature defiantly introduced resolutions calling for a state convention to take North Carolina out of the Confederacy. Opponents

Whether raiding government supplies or helping feed deserters among their kinfolk, women in the mountains increasingly turned against the Confederate war effort.
(SOURCE: *From J. Madison,* Fast and Loose in Dixie *(1880).*)

cried treason and blamed such talk for emboldening the Yankees. Desperately, the Confederate Congress enacted legislation permitting slaves to join the army as combat soldiers. Although such a policy was tantamount to emancipation, President Jefferson Davis urged it, leaving many slaveholders aghast.

The political debates were made all the more bitter by the unchecked spread of violence and desertion across the state. In Yadkin County women desperate for food raided Confederate granaries in January. Lizzie Lenoir described the raids to her aunt Sarah with the disapproval of one who was not facing starvation. The raiders were "*women*," she noted with disbelief. Armed with axes, they hoped to haul off the corn in the warehouses with wagons. While a guard at the Jamesville warehouse held them at bay, "an old drunk man" scared their horses into bolting. Lizzie was happy to report that "they didn't get any of the corn." Women raiding the Hamptonville warehouse were able to take away all the corn they wanted. Lizzie could explain their "unbecoming behavior" only by insisting that cowardly men, "*deserters* perhaps or distillers," put them up to it. She sadly concluded that "the degeneracy of the times is truly alarming."

Areas that avoided the worst of this "degeneracy" did so by resorting to the pragmatic expedient of arranging a truce between the warring factions. Word went out to the deserters around Caldwell County that they could return to their homes unmolested, provided they lived quietly and made an effort at restitution for the property they had pillaged.

Before the Caldwell County court finalized the truce, General George Stoneman's raiders tore through the county in the largest and most sustained Federal attack on western North Carolina.

The 6,000 Union cavalry left East Tennessee in late March for a monthlong raid aimed at disrupting Confederate communications, destroying military resources, and liberating the 10,000 Federal prisoners held in Salisbury, North Carolina. Under tight discipline when they entered Wilkes and Caldwell counties, the troops inflicted less damage on civilian property than had been feared. They "were not allowed to plunder to any great extent or commit any acts of violence," Joe Norwood reported. Still, the raid caught local residents by surprise and few had time to hide and guard their slaves and livestock in the surrounding woods. Once they knew that Federal troops were in the vicinity, many slaves had all the incentive they needed to escape. As Norwood wrote to Walter, "about two days before [Stoneman's men arrived] a considerable number of negro men left for Tennessee & have not been heard from since." Among those who made a bid for freedom were five of Norwood's and four of Rufus's from Fort Defiance.

The presence of Federal troops unleashed class tensions among whites as well as the latent conflicts between masters and slaves. For weeks, Norwood and other slaveholders had been "under constant apprehension about tory or robber bands & I have been serving on guard every third night & have been as much as two weeks without taking off my clothes," he wrote. Ironically, Norwood's property was more secure when Federal troops were in the neighborhood commanded by officers who looked to the local elite as their natural allies in maintaining social order and restoring political allegiance to the Union. That became apparent in the aftermath of the second occupation of the town of Lenoir in mid-April, when Stoneman stopped for two days in Lenoir to set up a temporary prison in Saint James Episcopal Church.

During the brief occupation guards were detailed to protect local homes, including Norwood's. Soon after the Federals pulled out, local marauders descended on the town, ransacking property the Federals had protected.

Not all of Stoneman's officers shared his concern for the property rights of Confederates. Many of the men serving under him, especially Southerners who had enlisted in the Union army after fleeing from their mountain homes, were thirsting for revenge against the elite whom they blamed for the war. In exacting it, they often had the assistance of slaves. According to Selina Norwood, Stoneman's men "tore everything to pieces at Uncle Avery's, put pistols to the ladies' heads, drove them out of the house and took what they liked, guided by a negro."

Little news from Tom and Walter out in Haywood reached Fort Defiance in the last months of the war. The constant threat of attack by pillaging deserters prevented Tom from making his regular mail runs to the post office in Asheville. While Tom stood guard, Walter was able to get away for a brief visit to Fort Defiance. On the way back, he began composing a series of anti-Yankee poems and patriotic Confederate songs that he passed on to friends and sent off to newspapers for publication. Even as Confederate defenses collapsed and the mountain society around him fragmented into rival kinship groupings intent only on survival, he never gave in to defeatism. "Don't suffer yourself to get blue" in those Petersburg trenches, he wrote his nephew Tom Norwood in March. "It is a Yankee color and does not become a Confederate soldier."

There was much to be blue about. In early May 1865, Tom and Walter got a taste of what their Avery relatives had endured two weeks earlier. In the backwash of the war Union cavalry came to Crab Orchard. Their visit hardened Walter's hatred of Yankees and his determination to remain an unreconstructed Confederate in the postwar period.

NOTES

Tom Norwood's reports to Walter of desertion in Lee's army touched on a growing problem in the Confederate military that is fully analyzed in Mark A. Weitz, *More Damning Than Slaughter: Desertion in the Confederate Army* (Lincoln: University of Nebraska Press, 2005). Paul D. Escott, *Many Excellent People: Power and Privilege in North Carolina, 1850–1900* (Chapel Hill: University of North Carolina Press, 1985), pp. 59–84, surveys the rising anti-Confederate sentiment in North Carolina that so concerned the Gwyns. John C. Inscoe and Gordon B. McKinney, *The Heart of Confederate Appalachia: Western North Carolina in the Civil War* (Chapel Hill: University of North Carolina Press, 2000); and *The Civil War in Appalachia: Collected Essays*, ed. Kenneth W. Noe and Shannon H. Wilson (Knoxville: University of Tennessee Press, 1997) explore in depth the breakdown of community and the outbreak of guerrilla warfare that wracked much of western North Carolina. For a well-balanced account of the divisions in one mountain community, see Martin Crawford, *Ashe County's Civil War: Community and Society in the Appalachian South* (Charlottesville: University of Virginia Press, 2001). The burdens of the war fell most heavily on workingwomen, and Victoria Bynum relates part of their story in *Unruly Women: The Politics of Social and Sexual Control in the Old South* (Chapel Hill: University of North Carolina Press, 1992). For a sensitive and harrowing fictional depiction of the turmoil in the Carolina mountains, see Charles Frazier, *Cold Mountain* (New York: Atlantic Monthly Press, 1997).

That North Carolina supplied men and material to the Confederacy until the very end was largely attributable to the astute wartime leadership of Governor Zebulon Vance. For Vance's governorship and the deft way in which he turned back the peace movement led by William W. Holden, see Gordon B. McKinney, *Zeb Vance: North Carolina's Civil War Governor and Gilded Age Political Leader* (Chapel Hill: University of North Carolina Press, 2004).

Despite savage beatings of slaves from masters such as the one Walter inflicted on Delia, African Americans were able to take advantage of the divisions among whites on the home front by slackening off the pace of their work, widening the boundaries of their autonomy, and fleeing behind Union lines whenever the opportunity beckoned. For the changing patterns of race relations unleashed by the war, Clarence Mohr, *On the Threshold of Freedom: Masters and Slaves in Civil War Georgia* (Athens: University of Georgia Press, 1986) remains unsurpassed. The broadest treatment of how slavery and the Confederate war effort were intertwined can be found in Armstead L. Robinson, *Bitter Fruits of Bondage: The Demise of Slavery and the Collapse of the Confederacy, 1861–1865* (Charlottesville: University of Virginia Press, 2005).

The evolving Union policy toward slaves that Walter to his surprise came to accept is traced out in *Slaves No More: Three Essays on Emancipation and the Civil War*, ed. Ira Berlin, Barbara J. Fields, Steven F. Miller, Joseph P. Reidy, and Leslie S. Rowland (New York: Cambridge University Press, 1992). These essays drew on the material in the same editors' magnificently descriptive series *Freedom: A Documentary History of Emancipation* (New York: Cambridge University Press, 1982–), an indispensable source on the role of African Americans in the war.

Five

UNRECONSTRUCTED CONFEDERATE

———*∿*———

LEE SURRENDERED AT APPOMATTOX COURT HOUSE ON APRIL 9, 1865; organized military resistance in North Carolina ended when General Joseph E. Johnston capitulated at Durham Station on April 26. Guerrilla skirmishes in the western mountains continued into early May, when another Federal regiment of mounted infantry rode into Haywood to clear out the guerrillas.

On May 2 Federal troops helped themselves to Tom' and Walter's possessions. Walter lost four bacon hams, a mule, and "old Rip," a horse that behaved so gently it seemed to understand the need to protect Walter's crippled leg. Many of the cavalry were "home Yankees," mountain Unionists recruited into the Federal army, who had a special grudge against neighbors like Tom who had spent much of the war hunting down Confederate deserters. Tom and Lizzie's house was searched and some of their personal possessions carried off, as well as horses, mules, and hams. Tom had to swallow his pride when he was forced to stand back while Lizzie's pockets were searched.

Despite the "overthrow of our country" and the end of slavery, Walter was surprisingly buoyant about the future. Whereas most slaveholders were demoralized and depressed as they faced the need for new labor arrangements to replace slavery, Walter had always insisted that he never wanted to own slaves because of the "peculiar institution's" moral evils. Unable on his own to cut free from slave ownership, he was relieved that Yankee emancipation had made up his mind for him. Now the South was in a position to take up the system of free labor development he had always favored. A new, progressive South of white independent farmers and enterprising businessmen could finally emerge.

A few days after the Union cavalry left Crab Orchard, Walter met with his former slaves and told them he no longer wanted them around. He offered Andy, who had been his most trusted slave, a chance to stay on if he would do so "on the same terms as heretofore"—as a slave in practice, if not in name. But under no circumstances would Walter hire Andy or rent land to him. To Walter's "great relief," Andy left and rented a cabin for his family from a white farmer about two miles up the creek. Walter's other former slaves soon crowded into the cabin with Andy's family. Walter was so anxious to see them go that he gave them his best cow, three hogs, sixteen bushels of corn, some tools, and over 100 pounds of bacon. He had been so generous, he explained to Joe Norwood, because he wanted his "hands washed of all further responsibility for the maintenance of Africans." He did not notice, of course, that these "Africans" had been maintaining him, but he felt free to dispense with their labor now that returning veterans and mountain families impoverished by the war provided a plentiful supply of cheap hired hands. So many whites returned to Haywood at the end of the war that Walter had to turn away many seeking work.

Unlike Walter, most slaveholders in Haywood tried to hold on to the old order by treating emancipation as a mere formality. After first refusing to negotiate terms with their freed people, they soon gave in out of economic necessity. Confronted with black demands for autonomy and their own pressing need for workers, they reluctantly entered into a series of ad hoc contractual agreements. Tom Lenoir, for example, worked out an arrangement under which his former slaves would have to "behave well & work faithfully & according to my directions until the corn was cribbed." In return, he agreed to "give them" one-third of the corn, one-tenth of the wheat, and half of the potatoes, buckwheat, and molasses. In addition, he would furnish them with their food provisions and enough raw wool and cotton for making their annual clothing allotment. He wrote out two copies of his "promises," signed them before a witness, gave his workers one copy, and kept the other.

By summer's end Tom was uncertain if he wanted to enter into another labor agreement. With the exception of Mary, who felt she was overworked and left, all his former slaves had stayed on. He was pleased enough with the men but complained that "the wenches have behaved badly & I am heartily tired of some of them." What most worried him was that many of the slaves in the neighborhood who had fled during the war were returning and looking for work. Fearful that he would be surrounded by a band of thieves, he told his black hands that if any of them encouraged others to settle in the area, he "would cut loose from the whole concern" and drive them all away.

Tom assumed that any black released from the discipline of slavery would have to steal from whites in order to survive—a common view among Southern whites. In combating the antislavery attacks of the outside world, they had convinced themselves that blacks were an inferior race that was naturally unfit for free labor. Responding to reports that blacks in Asheville were stealing from their former masters to supply the shiftless, improvident blacks who had struck out on their own, Walter commented that "it is very natural that such a state of affairs should arise."

"Get rid of your negroes as soon as possible," Walter advised Joe Norwood and Rufus. Perhaps they should even dismiss their white tenants. Their most valuable assets were their land and timber, both of which would be abused by tenant farmers. Shifting their plantation operations into stock raising and pasturage would minimize the need for labor and promote rising land values. Such was Walter's strategy for Crab Orchard. If enough mountain farmers followed his course, "the material development of our up country will be very rapid, and those who own plenty of land and can take care of it and pay the taxes will soon find themselves growing rich."

Few former slaveholders shared Walter's optimism. The twin blows of defeat and emancipation had shattered the basis of their prewar prosperity and left them with devastating losses. But for Walter slavery had always been a burden. Part of him could welcome defeat for removing the main stumbling block to the moral and economic advancement of the South. After all, slavery had saddled his father at Fort Defiance with a wasteful labor system and shiftless black workers. At Crab Orchard he was free of both his slaves and the black presence he had always dreaded.

Walter was also cheered by new living arrangements that were "infinitely more pleasant" than life with his slaves. As soon as

Andy left with his family, Walter opened up the slaves' cabin to the sun and rain. A week later, he scoured it with boiling water before moving in. He then moved one of his tenants, Jesse R. Anderson, into his old cabin, where Anderson and his sister provided board for Walter and his day laborer. He characterized the Andersons in terms he never applied to his slaves: "honest, sensible, industrious, quiet, neat." Knowing that white tenants could easily be replaced, he preferred working with them, rather than the slaves who required constant supervision or punishment. Fortunately the Union raid in May had missed "one good mule," which had been on loan to a neighbor. Walter was still able to get in a "promising" crop of corn.

Looking beyond Crab Orchard, Walter also assumed that the Union would allow the ruling class of the South to control its own affairs. His optimism seemed reasonable in the summer and fall of 1865. Although President Andrew Johnson had appointed Walter's political enemy William Holden as North Carolina's provisional governor, Holden moved cautiously in reorganizing the state government. He appointed many noted opponents of secession to his administration, but nonetheless he relied on the advice of notable local leaders, like Walter's cousin, Rufus Lenoir Patterson of Caldwell County. Above all, Holden opposed granting civic and political equality to the freed population. Jonathan Worth, a former Whig Unionist who defeated Holden in the gubernatorial election held in November 1865, promised to be more even more conservative.

One threat to the "quiet times" Walter enjoyed in Haywood was the Brownlow movement in Tennessee. A Methodist circuit rider and Knoxville newspaper editor before the war, William

G. Brownlow was Tennessee's most noted and powerful Unionist. Elected governor in March 1865 under a new state constitution that allowed only Unionists to vote, he announced that Confederates could expect no leniency from him. In the following months Tennessee Unionists set out to punish their rebel neighbors and clogged the courts with damage suits seeking to recover wartime property losses. Walter feared that the same "devilish element" was emerging in Haywood and that he and his friends would be plunged "into a living purgatory" by the "most worthless men in the country...who suppose that every rebel in the land is liable to every tory and every Yankee for damages for sustaining the war in behalf of the South."

Brownlow's give-no-quarter politics sank only shallow roots in North Carolina, and its worst excesses had passed in Tennessee by 1866. David M. Key, a Lenoir cousin and prominent secessionist from East Tennessee who had been hunted and almost killed by Unionists in the last months of the war, received a special pardon from President Johnson in May 1865 and resumed his law practice in Chattanooga in the fall of 1865. He wrote Rufus in January that "I have got along as well as I could have hoped for...Union men, even the most bitter, employ me, as well as those who have been rebels." In fact, his legal business boomed, largely because of the flood of suits against rebels for wartime damages. Most were quickly settled in favor of the defendants, and treason charges against Key and other leading Confederates were dropped.

In December, however, the large Republican majority in Congress refused to seat the congressional delegations elected under Johnson's guidelines for quickly restoring former Confederate states to the Union. Many Southern elites viewed the Republicans' action as a prelude to extending political rights to the freedmen. Once their former slaves had the vote, the upper classes fully expected a new political majority to form consisting of the freedmen and the poor whites who had openly defied the authority of the elites during the war. If that occurred, would revenge be long in coming?

By the end of the year Walter's optimism had given way to foreboding. In addition to losing confidence that the Republicans would leave men of his class undisturbed in their control of the state, he was seeing increasing signs that his lower-class neighbors around Crab Orchard were finding common cause with the freed slaves—an alliance of the "whiskey and colored people," he called them. To his horror, "some of my nearest neighbors have bowed down before the ebony idol and are worshiping it with the zeal of new converts." Two weeks later, he described his situation to Sarah as "rather cheerless just now. The East Fork is to be the negro colony of Haywood, and I in the midst of it." The blacks he wanted to be free of were apparently closing in on him, and he was convinced that some of his white neighbors had sunk to such "a very low ebb" in their "morality and virtue" as to welcome the black presence. He had always felt settled at Crab Orchard, but now he was considering "giving all up."

In the winter of 1865–1866, most of the Lenoirs and their friends were as despondent as Walter. Rufus faced a quandary as he tried to make plans for his farming operations in the spring. "I feel like a man in a swamp on a dark night, no place to rest— afraid to stand still and wait for light on my path—afraid to move without even the light of a star to guide me." Tom was equally depressed. He cut off most of his correspondence, canceled his newspaper subscriptions, and barely budged from his farm. His former slaves had left in the fall, and he doubted whether he would be able to make enough by farming to pay his three hired hands, support his wife and child, and discharge his debts. He had been relying on the cotton he purchased early in the war and on a note of $1,500 owed him by J. W. Patton to clear his debts, but Patton's heavy wartime losses left his estate insolvent and Sherman's troops burned his cotton. Tom was forced to sell his bacon to raise cash, which he planned to use for badly needed farm repairs.

In coping with what Walter's sister Mary Ann characterized as a "maze of doubt and fear," the Lenoirs consoled themselves with the fact that they were no longer responsible for their slaves. "As far as I am personally concerned the breaking up of the 'institution' is rather a relief to my mind," wrote Mary Ann, agreeing with Walter; "if we could only get *rid* of the negroes, but, there is the *rub*! ... I have served a pretty long apprenticeship to ours and would be glad to be free of them." Her only regret was that as a "professing Christian" she had not done more for "the welfare of their souls." Although she had relied on her female slaves to wet-nurse her children when she herself was too ill to feed them, she saw herself as a long-suffering martyr to spoiled slaves who "had grown so fond of style and fashion they were mostly an expense any way." They were "nothing more to [her] now than other free *niggars*." Whatever befell them now was none of her concern. Her conscience was clean: "*I* did not make them slaves [and] I don't think there ever was a more hellish act committed by any nation than this emancipation in the manner in which they have done it ... Well, well, on their heads be the sin."

Tom and Walter also took the moral high ground in asserting that the Yankees had freed the slaves "not from any real desire to benefit the negro, or truly philanthropic motives" but out of "avarice, envy, hatred, & malice." In an argument echoed more formally by Southern theologians, Tom maintained that the destruction of slavery in no way registered God's moral condemnation of the institution. God had ordained the "wicked" to end slavery not because the institution was inherently sinful, but because individual slaveholders had proved unworthy of their moral responsibility as masters.

Although agreeing with Tom that the Yankees had freed the slaves only as "a last resort" in a desperate strategy to win the war, Walter saw no need to use religion to defend slavery—an institution he had judged as wrong "in the abstract." Still, white Southerners needed to set the record straight and make certain that the North did not unjustly convert its military victory into a moral one. Walter suppressed what he himself had clearly recognized prior to Lincoln's call for troops—that the states of the original Confederacy had seceded to defend slavery against the inroads of antislavery Northerners. Even in the Upper South, slaveholders had provided secession with its original support. But with the Confederacy in ashes, Walter put slavery in the background. The "South fought this war in self defense against unwarranted and unprovoked assaults upon her constitutional rights," he insisted. Slavery had little to do with the war until the Yankees cynically embarked on emancipation to gain more troops and win the approval of the outside world. Although the result of the war was "disastrous," he believed that Southerners had not fought in vain. They "made a proud record [and] established a high national character (for we are as separate people, and will be)." As crushing as defeat had been, "such a war with such an ending is better for us than tame submission would have been." This was the version of the war that he had faith "history will finally record."

Walter also gave much thought to the "social revolution" he believed the South was about to undergo in the wake of its defeat. "It is very odious," he wrote his sister Sarah in January 1866, "but the rising and future generations of the South must be more or less yankeeized." By that he meant a coarsening of manners and the rise of new and vulgar moneyed classes. Like so many Confederates trying to make sense out of their defeat, he romanticized the Southern past to make it worthy of the blood and treasure spent in an effort to preserve it. Although slavery had "defects of the greatest character," he praised the institution for securing "to the cultivated white people of the South a social organization productive of more genial warmth, ease of manner, refinement, and virtue than existed at the North, or perhaps among a whole people in any other country." The Old South, as he now remembered it, never required mere wealth as an entrée to the better sort of society. Indeed, "in no country was wealth of any sort as little requisite as a passport to society." He seemed to forget that before the war he had been so disenchanted with the South that he was on the verge of moving to Minnesota.

But the old order was already changing, Walter told Sarah, for wealth was all the Yankee victors cared about. Although the "good old school" of Southern ladies and gentlemen would not disappear entirely, Walter predicted that "our poor white people will soon find themselves galled by the presence among us of at least two other higher classes who have been little known among us as yet." One would constitute a "shoddy aristocracy," those whose sudden wealth outpaced their refinement, who would assume haughty airs as they drove hard bargains with their white laborers. The other new class, the "very wealthy and extravagant devotees of fashion," would ape the titled aristocracy of Europe and separate themselves from the masses in a dazzling display of their wealth. Competition for jobs and advancement would be fierce in Walter's Yankeeized South, and the main losers would be the poor of both races who had lost their benefactors in the old master class. As these new classes increased in size and power, the position of the poor would deteriorate until "the poor will barely be able by hard work to live and will perish from want when unable to work."

In sketching this grim scenario, Walter urged Sarah to consider how it related to "the very practical subject of the employment of labor at the South for house and farm work, and on various questions of economy associated with it." As large landowners, the Lenoirs had to hire labor in order to earn a productive return on their land and leave an economic legacy for their children. But whom to hire? Blacks were accustomed to plantation routines, but they were habitual thieves who would never be self-supporting as long as they had access to "the old crib and smokehouse." Native whites could be hired cheaply, but they had few skills and would resent being given the kind of orders a slave would take. No doubt foreign-born whites would prove to be reliable and productive, but how many could be recruited in upcountry North Carolina? Walter preferred northern Europeans, especially the Scots, who were noted for their thriftiness.

This labor question confronted the Lenoirs and their relatives just after the war. The question of whether to employ black hands was resolved for many of them when their former slaves simply walked off. Most blacks left Fort Defiance in the spring of 1865. While Rufus was rounding up some hired hands to work in the fields, he and Sarah did all the housework. Hearing that some black families were emigrating to the western mountains, Sallie Lenoir wrote to Tom's wife in January 1866, warning them to be on the alert against Haywood becoming "a darkey colony." She also reported that Polly, one of those rare freed slaves who had been "very correct in her deportment all along," was about to leave with her husband George to farm on a small plot of land Rufus had agreed to rent to them. Since none of the local white women met Sallie's standards for a house servant, she and Rufus would do the cooking, milking, and housekeeping once Polly was gone. Although they had one former slave woman who did their washing and "any sort of drudgery," they thought it best "to try to do without Darkies awhile."

At first Walter applauded the resolve of the Lenoir women at Fort Defiance to manage their household without outside help. But by the fall of 1866, he was urging them to hire "one or two good [white] female employees." Surely they had more profitable ways to spend their days than "in the mere manual labor of the establishment," and enough time had passed for "some new ideas to dawn upon the laboring classes of the South," namely, that there was no stigma in working for a well-situated family that could pay them well. Tom's wife had found three reliable single white women. He advised Sarah and Sallie to give preference to white women "over twenty, of established character, and not from the immediate neighborhood." Apparently he feared that young girls from around Fort Defiance would be too prone to gossip to their friends about the Lenoirs or run back home if reprimanded.

In truth, Sarah and Sallie were desperate for any help they could get. "It is so 'lonesome' here the darkies are not willing to come," Sarah reported in November, "and the white women have got a wrong kink in their heads some way, and I don't believe it will come out soon." Cousin Betsey up in Elkin knew of one black woman but felt she was "too slow." Slow or not, Sarah was willing to give her a try for "we would gladly hire help if we could."

Notwithstanding Sarah's eagerness, complaints about white laborers were as common after the war as the assertion that blacks would not work without the guiding hand of their former masters. Once their freed people either left or were driven off, many planters had no choice but to turn for labor to "white trash," as they now called them, whom they had always viewed as their social inferiors. No longer isolated from poor whites and now suddenly forced to depend on them, planters experienced a form of culture shock.

Lizzie Key, Walter's cousin in Loudon, Tennessee, was distressed by the awful conditions she and her family faced on her plantation. The slaves had run off when Yankee raiders came through and about a dozen white families, "a perfectly worthless and trifling population," had taken their place. "There is not an honest one among them," Lizzie complained to Sallie Lenoir. "They pretend to rent land but take all sorts of advantages and cheat as much as possible." Particularly galling was the behavior of the three families living in the cabins previously used by the slaves. Against the express wishes of Lizzie's mother, they persisted in opening the gates to the front yard and allowing the pigs and hogs to roam at will. Her mother chased them out in the morning and the tenants let them back in at night. The yard looked like an "old field" with its uprooted grass and trampled flowers. The Yankees had pillaged so successfully that her mother was "dependent now on this *trash* here in the yard to haul her wood—she has no wagons, no harness—they bring her wood that is not fit to burn and they have plenty of the best wood all the time."

Accustomed to unquestioned obedience from their slaves, planters railed against the assertiveness of their new laborers and tenants regardless of their race. This new labor was "demoralized," as they put it. Unable to decide who was worse—whites or blacks—they experimented with both. Julia Reagan, another Lenoir cousin from East Tennessee, had tried with her mother to find a suitable white girl to do housework, but as soon as any of them made enough money "to buy…a little finery they want to quit working." They now had a "very good '*freed woman*' from N.C. [who was] a very good cook, washer & ironer &c." Even Walter, who hired all the white hands he needed at fifty cents a day in the first year after the war, began employing blacks in 1867. Even more surprising, given his prior disparagement of black laborers, he found them to be "good and faithful hands." James Gwyn alternated the employment of black and white hands every other year, in order, as his son explained to Walter, "to see which will do best." Racial etiquette also played a role in Gwyn's decision not to employ a racially mixed crew. "We think it best to have all the hirelings of a colour," he noted to Tom; "it does not suit to have white women in the kitchen cooking & negro boys, or men, there to eat."

No matter the race of his hands or renters, Gwyn made little progress in restoring the prewar income from his plantation.

He had been of a mind in 1866 to pull up stakes and buy some good grazing land in the Shenandoah Valley, where he would be free of his "mean & trifling" white neighbors, but he stuck it out and continued to feel stymied. He confessed to Rufus in 1868 that he was at a loss as to how best to manage his land. "I find to rent to negroes I get very little & it's poorly cultivated, not atal [*sic*] improved, but damaged; & I judge it would be nearly, or quite as bad if I were to rent it to white people & they would likely have more stock to annoy me." Hiring hands to cultivate his land barely paid with the prevailing prices of corn and bacon, but he had no choice if he wanted to earn enough to meet expenses and pay taxes. He would have preferred to leave most of his land uncultivated in an effort to restore its fertility, but that still would have required hired hands to keep out briars and broom straw and he could not afford to give up what limited income he derived from his corn and hogs. "I reckon it best to do part of both," he told Rufus, "rent a part & let a part rest." Rufus faced the same quandary.

Living in the western mountains where soil and climate were more favorable to stock raising and grass cultivation (which minimized the need for labor), Walter was more optimistic about his prospects. Sarah, lonely after the death of her mother, begged her "dear" Walter to come back to Fort Defiance. Her brother had been "the companion and playmate of my childhood, the pride of my girlhood and the sympathizing friend of my womanhood." If he returned, she would care for him as she had for her mother. But Walter insisted that Crab Orchard was the best place for him. No doubt living with Sarah and Rufus in his boyhood home would be very "desirable and suitable," but he was "so selfish that

I must have something of my own to work for and to care for and to plan for." That something was his farm at Crab Orchard and the plans he had for it. He needed a goal and the challenge of working toward it in order to feel contented and useful. Even if worse came to worst and he had to leave, his "same restless desire to have something to do" would most likely lead him to a town or city where his disabled condition could still allow him to engage in some business pursuit. All he could offer Sarah in consolation was the reflection that as he lay sick and dying, "I will probably see the matter just as you do."

As he continued to deny himself the warmth and affection of his remaining family at Fort Defiance, Walter found companionship in nature. Living and working on his mountain farm was therapeutic. One of his greatest pleasures was caring for his animals and watching the progression of the seasons in a nearly pristine wilderness. He spoke of "a kind of companionship" with "what we call the inferior animals and the vegetables ... as they live and move and grow." He struck the tone of a Thoreau in recalling "listening at the birds, and watching the gambols of the squirrels and the graceful motion of the fish, in gentling and handling my stock of all kinds, and in watching the growth and development of my crops and young fruit trees and my flowers and shrubs." He had no desire to be anyplace else and seldom ventured even as far as Tom's cabin just down the road.

He tried to avoid even thinking about politics. Citing his distance from the state capital in Raleigh and the difficulty of traveling with only one leg, he turned down his unsolicited appointment as a counselor of state for Governor Worth in 1865. He did not even know whether he would bother to vote on the state's proposed new constitution, which followed President Johnson's guidelines in repudiating the doctrine of secession and acknowledging the legal end of slavery. In determining the number of seats in the lower branch of the state legislature, the new constitution dropped what was known as the Federal ratio under which a slave counted as three-fifths of a white person. Instead, only whites were counted in apportioning representation. County officials, previously appointed for life by the governor, were to be popularly elected for a fixed term of six years. In all other respects, the new constitution was a very conservative document. Property qualifications continued for state officeholders and the freed blacks could neither vote nor hold office. Walter cared "but little" for the amendments on secession and emancipation. Only the changes on the basis of representation and the election of magistrates, both of which were supported in the overwhelmingly white western counties, met with his approval.

Walter did plan on voting for the "Southern candidates" in the October state elections in an effort to ensure that the state legislature rejected the proposed Fourteenth Amendment that the Republican Congress had approved in June. The amendment extended full citizenship to the former slaves and denied the right to hold public office to members of the South's old ruling class who had voluntarily supported the Confederacy. Walter denounced the amendment for its "degradation of the white race and the disfranchisement of the best part of it." If forced on the South, "we will have to accept it as a part of our fate; but to give our own consent and sanction to such dishonor and outrage...would be a burning shame not to be thought of by a man of independent spirit."

Detecting an improvement in the behavior of his neighbors, Walter felt that Haywood was experiencing "very peaceable times" by the summer of 1866. He attributed it to a decline in drinking and in trespassing on private land. He still feared a lurking "spirit of evil"—the "secret ill will of the radicals for the decent men." Led by Holden, this white minority favored ratification of the Fourteenth Amendment. To Walter's alarm, ministers from the northern Methodist Church were organizing radicals in the western mountains. In 1844 the Methodist Episcopal Church had split into separate institutions in the North and South over the slavery issue. Convinced that the peace and welfare of their church and their country required the South to accept the terms of the Fourteenth Amendment, the northern Methodist bishops strongly backed Congress in its struggle against Johnson and launched an aggressive campaign to win back Southern Methodists and regain control of church property in the South. Their greatest success came in the mountains of East Tennessee and western North Carolina. They recruited members with such zeal and effectiveness in Haywood that Walter feared the county was about to be taken over by "a mere political machine, a powerful radical political organization, thoroughly drilled and disciplined as such, its political tactics thoroughly systematized in every thing from Sunday School up."

Another factor that kept mountain radicalism alive, Walter believed, was the "delusion still existing in the minds of the ignorant portion of the radicals that they will be able to confiscate our lands." During the war Unionists in Tennessee and Missouri had passed laws allowing the lands of Confederates to be confiscated. Although any such law had been expressly prohibited in North

Carolina by a provision in the state constitution, Walter was convinced that the rebel leaders were telling their followers that rebel estates were soon to be confiscated.

Walter warned that the radicals would violate all standards of reason and decency in their "hunger" for rebel land: "they would accept negro equality, negro citizenship, negro office holding, would vote with the negro, vote for the negro, eat with him, sleep with him and miscegenate with him, if it would help them, or if they thought it would help them to share of the good rebel land" they crave. The first signs of a biracial alliance among the rural poor made Walter fear that lower-class whites harbored burning resentment against the elite that once ruled North Carolina and carried it into the disastrous war against the North. He advised Rufus to follow his policy of "commendable hypocrisy" in public dealings with the radicals. Rather than shunning them, he would treat them with a studied politeness to avoid further inflaming their animosity.

Walter's low regard for the white radicals encouraged him to think that the freedmen would break off their alliance and return to their true friends, the rebels in the old planter class. After all, the planters had always looked out for the welfare of blacks, he believed. Walter was quick to pass on to Rufus reports that those who "called themselves good union men" were cheating the freedmen out of their work while the former rebels were offering better terms for their labor and scrupulously abiding by them. The worst offenders among the radicals, according to Walter, were those with the poorest land. From what he had heard, they were planning on bringing in unsuspecting black families to clear their land and then releasing them without pay once the work was done.

Even the radicals' religious practices struck Walter as evidence of moral decay and a flouting of decency. To him, Methodist revivals seemed an excuse for sexual licentiousness. The shouting and the "grand and lofty trembling" at the nightly meetings served only as a release for the basest of passions. As proof, he related to Rufus the story of a young white couple who married in the summer of 1866, some seven months after they both had been active in a revival. She was visibly pregnant, and "if gossip for once tells the truth she was not the only white sister that ran the risk of such an accident." Gossip among black women at the revival told of "colored sisters" similarly impregnated though they "have not been so fortunate yet as to procure husbands to reward them for it." Such, concluded Walter primly, was "poor human nature."

These same "radical" stirrings convinced Walter's cousin William Bingham that the "Yankees are gone mad." Like most Southern whites, Bingham had hoped the South could prevent black suffrage by rejecting the Fourteenth Amendment and turning to President Johnson for protection. He quickly changed his mind. By the summer of 1866, he realized that "the masses of the North are with Congress, and that the most the President can do is to protect himself from impeachment, if he can do that. The people are worse than Congress, & the clergy are worse than the people." Once the fall elections gave the Republicans an even greater majority in Congress, he saw no way of turning back the tide. "*Liberty is gone forever*; it took its last flight when Lee surrendered," he lamented. Bingham did detect "one hopeful sign." Outraged Southern whites were "beginning to have what we never had before, a Southern nationality."

Walter, of course, had been an unbending Southern nationalist from the moment he decided to enlist in the Confederate army. A letter from Sarah in the fall of 1866 renewed all the pride he felt for the sacrifices made on behalf of his South. George, one of the family's former slaves, had caught his arm in a cane mill, and Sarah and Rufus watched in horror as it was amputated. To her surprise, she empathized with George's pain as a fellow human being. "I never expected to feel for Negroes as I felt for him and his wife. We feel as if our *friends* were in distress." They immediately thought of their beloved brother Walter and "wondered as we have many times before, how you did live through it!" She cried in thinking of what he had endured. "I don't know that Stone Wall Jackson has a sister, if he had she is no prouder of him that I am of *my brother*! Didn't you suffer in a good cause, a cause none the *less dear to a woman's heart that it is a lost one*! And you are the only one of *us* that did fight too!"

Reading this, Walter wept and could not help thinking of his marriage to sweet Nealy. He wrote of the "sacred duty" he had discharged during the war as the response of a man's heart to a woman's love and vowed that he had no regrets over having lost a leg in showing his love. As a token of his love for Sarah, he hoped soon to invite her to visit Crab Orchard so she could savor the views from the new home he was building. Completing the house, like all the other farmwork, would be arduous, but Walter was not "yet so old or so crippled as not to feel the instructive impulse which prompts a man to love to cope with difficulties and to overcome them." Out of that same pride he derived satisfaction from his fumbling attempts to perform the endless manual labor on his farm. He had come to realize that "one of the greatest sources of my pleasure in them is their very difficulty."

As to politics and the future of the South, Walter urged Sarah not to be unduly alarmed. The South, having rejected the Fourteenth Amendment, was doing just fine outside of the Union and "if we don't beg in, will soon be begged in." He was also happy to hear that two African Americans had just been elected to the legislature in Massachusetts. For Walter, black political activity was always inseparable from a sexual mixing of the races, and he now looked forward with a malicious glee to seeing the Yankees have a taste of their own medicine. If only the two Massachusetts legislators were "black negroes, instead of the bright mulattoes that they no doubt are, and that they were married to two Massachusetts white females."

During the autumn of 1866 Walter built a log stable and finished his fencing and road projects. He was turning his cornfields over to pasture as fast as he could and adding additional pasture by planting timothy and redtop on his thin upland soils. His new house would have to wait until the completion of a sawmill that would provide him with his lumber. But he was happy. "I was never before so entirely devoted to any occupation or business as I am now to the improvement and cultivation of my farm," he wrote Sarah.

Walter's decision to forge ahead at Crab Orchard left his friends and family dumbfounded. "What folly, for a man of his fine sense & his helpless condition to think of such a thing," an incredulous James Gwyn wrote Rufus. He urged Tom to persuade Walter to give up his foolish notions and return to "the old homestead where he would be a comfort to his friends & live a life of ease & pleasure." Not seeing how Walter could ever make his farm productive or live comfortably in the wilds of Haywood, Gwyn thought he should rent his lands and return home. But in the early spring of 1867 Walter set out on an audacious new path that would change the course of his life.

He had returned to Fort Defiance on his most extended stay since leaving four years earlier. What brought him back was a meeting of the heirs to his brother William's still unsettled estate. The bulk of it consisted of thousands of acres of land William had accumulated in three decades of speculation. Following Walter's advice, Rufus had taken the land off the market during the war and few buyers had emerged after the war. As the only lawyer among the heirs, Walter was the obvious choice to pore over the title papers and other documents needed to prepare the land for sale.

As he studied the documents, Walter began to mull over an idea. Rather than organizing the records so that each heir could sell his or her shares of William's land, Walter proposed to buy out his brothers and sisters and assume sole responsibility for selling the land. Over the next few months he persuaded five other heirs to accept his offer of $3,000 in specie equivalent for each of their shares. The sixth heir, Sarah, agreed to accept a note from Walter for the $3,000. In order to gain ownership of William's land, Walter had assumed a debt of $18,000, a tremendous sum in the cash-starved postwar South, easily equivalent to a small fortune.

Walter's decision to assume such a tremendous debt astounded his relatives as much as had his stubborn insistence on living in isolation at Crab Orchard. Though Walter did not say as much openly, he justified his decision by convincing himself that it was in the best interests of the family. As he worked through William's records, he quickly realized that legal title to much of the land could be disputed. Unless he undertook the arduous work of establishing those titles, the heirs might well face endless litigation and would wind up with very little for their shares. He was also concerned with meddling by his sister Laura's husband, Joe Norwood. The Lenoirs had never trusted Norwood's business sense, and Walter had little doubt that unless he stepped in Norwood would connive to sell Laura's share of the estate to the first bidder and use the proceeds to pay off his debts and engage in fresh speculation.

By paying what he considered a fair price for the land, Walter was providing his siblings with the ready cash they desperately needed in the uncertain times after the war. He was also honoring the memory of his troubled brother William, who had taken his own life. William had dreamed of accumulating vast landholdings to serve as a reserve that landless whites could draw on to begin lifting themselves up to lead productive lives of economic independence. William would show them the way by offering them land on easy terms and guiding them into becoming thrifty farmers. Walter shared William's dream. But to make it a reality, Walter needed control of all of William's land. Through its sale, Walter was certain he could create a model of economic development and moral uplift that would vindicate a white South so long maligned and degraded by the Yankee North.

Once he made up his mind, he knew that his life had taken a decisive turn. The work involved in surveying the land and clearing title likely meant scaling back or abandoning his farm at Crab

Orchard. "It will be the dearest sacrifice that I ever voluntarily made except going to the war," he wrote Tom in late March 1867, "and I did that much more cheerfully than I can enter upon this." He had no way of knowing just how much that sacrifice would entail.

NOTES

Apart from the opening chapters in Dan T. Carter, *When the War Was Over: The Failure of Self-Reconstruction in the South, 1865–1867* (Baton Rouge: Louisiana State University Press, 1985), little systematic work has been done on the chaotic conditions in the South at the end of the war. The range of emotions Southerners experienced as the Confederacy collapsed are insightfully described by Stephen V. Ash in *A Year in the South: Four Lives in 1865* (New York: Palgrave Macmillan, 2002). As Kenneth M. Stampp has argued in "The Southern Road to Appomattox," in *The Imperiled Union: Essays on the Background of the Civil War* (New York: Oxford University Press, 1980), some planters undoubtedly shared Walter's moral qualms over slavery and felt a sense of relief when it was ended. Most, however, seemed to fit the pattern of sullen resignation outlined in James L. Roark, *Masters without Slaves: Southern Planters in the Civil War and Reconstruction* (New York: Norton, 1977). Eugene D. Genovese, *A Consuming Fire: The Fall of the Confederacy in the Mind of the White Christian South* (Athens: University of Georgia Press, 1998) examines the reaction of Southern theologians to emancipation. For the end of slavery from the perspective of the enslaved, see Leon F. Litwack, *Been in the Storm So Long: The Aftermath of Slavery* (New York: Knopf, 1979).

In the spring of 1865 Walter and Tom confronted the issue that most concerned white Southerners—the need to fashion new work arrangements in the absence of slavery. The struggle to define and control the meaning of freedom and the labor relations that would accompany that freedom are outlined in Eric Foner, *Nothing but Freedom: Emancipation and Its Legacy* (Baton Rouge: Louisiana State University Press, 1983). Julie Saville, *The Work of Reconstruction: From Slave to Wage Laborer in South Carolina, 1860–1870* (New York: Cambridge University Press, 1994) is the most thorough study for any Southern state. Regarding North Carolina, see Sharon Ann Holt, *Making Freedom Pay: North Carolina Freed People Working for Themselves, 1865–1900* (Athens: University of Georgia Press, 2000).

The politics of presidential Reconstruction in North Carolina are best covered in two biographies, Richard L. Zuber, *Jonathan Worth: A Biography of a Southern Unionist* (Chapel Hill: University of North Carolina Press, 1965); and William C. Harris, *William Woods Holden: Firebrand of North Carolina Politics* (Baton Rouge: Louisiana State University Press, 1987). Race relations just after the war are treated in Roberta S. Alexander, *North Carolina Confronts the Freedmen: Race Relations during Presidential Reconstruction, 1865–1867* (Durham, N.C.: Duke University Press, 1985). On the religious side of Reconstruction that Walter found so baffling and threatening, see Daniel W. Stowell, *Rebuilding Zion: The Religious Reconstruction of the South, 1863–1877* (New York: Oxford University Press, 1998); and Reginald Hildebrand, *The Times Were Strange and Stirring: Methodist Preachers and the Crisis of Emancipation* (Durham, N.C.: Duke University Press, 1995).

· *Six* ·

LAND PROMOTER AND DREAMER

⁓

J UST AS WALTER WAS DECIDING TO GO INTO DEBT AND EMBARK
on a new career as a land promoter, the Radical Republicans in
Congress seized control of postwar policy. Provoked when the
former Confederate states rejected the Fourteenth Amendment
(only Tennessee ratified it), Congress in March 1867 required
that black suffrage be included in new state constitutions. The
vote of the freedmen, coupled with the temporary disfranchisement of those Confederates barred from holding office (by the
Fourteenth Amendment), allowed Republican parties to spring
up throughout the former Confederacy. Swept into office by the
vote of the freedmen and poor whites, especially in mountainous areas that had turned against Confederate policies, these new
parties accepted the terms set down by Congress and were in
power when their states were readmitted to the Union.

Most whites greeted black suffrage with stunned anger. Writing to Tom from Fort Defiance on March 31, Walter reported that
the whites seemed "to bear their political fate with the dignified
calmness appropriate to the circumstances." Two days later, a

Union army officer mounted the courthouse steps in Wilkesboro to announce the congressional demands. "He told us all we had to submit to the acts of Congress," reported James Gwyn, "& a heap of stuff about who carried on the war." It was, Gwyn added, "a great time for the tories & negroes."

Undeterred by the new political environment, Walter pushed ahead with his plans for William's land. After arranging with the other heirs for new deeds to be drawn up assigning him ownership of their shares, he spent most of the spring and summer on surveying expeditions. He began with the Beech Creek lands in Watauga that lay close to the Tennessee border. The soil here was poor and the tract was steep and heavily timbered. To expedite its sale, he created seventeen small lots priced at slightly under a dollar per acre. He had no wish to return to the area anytime soon. Not only was it remote, most of its settlers were poor Unionists, some of whom were trespassing on Walter's land. Not wanting to stir up trouble, he did his best to ingratiate himself with the local landowners, even though they were "a rough set, and some of them behaved very badly during the war, robbing even their poorest neighbors, and of course are still radicals." Many had "a bountiful supply of body lice, which have never been disbanded since the war," which, to Walter's dismay, were soon tormenting him too. He and his surveyor, A. C. Farthing, were more successful in fending off what Walter referred to as the "local body guard" of lice when they moved south in Watauga to survey a 500-acre tract adjoining the lands of Phillip Shull. By June, Walter was back in Caldwell County subdividing William's lands near Lenoir. Energized by his plans, he was hiking on his wooden leg up to ten miles a day over rough terrain and was not "atall broken down." He was beginning to think, as he wrote Tom, that he had made " a very good trade, perhaps too good a one, to buy the land at $18,000."

Walter remained optimistic even as political power in North Carolina was about to shift to the new Republican coalition of freedmen, disaffected white Unionists, and the handful of the white elite who had decided to cooperate with the Republicans in order to protect their property interests. Although he had made no land sales, he was certain his low prices would attract buyers. If he could borrow enough money to tide him over, he was "not afraid to wait awhile with the main bulk of the land." However, he had to admit that it seemed "as if the whole country were for sale; and the spirit of emigration from the state is one of the worst signs for us."

Gwyn needed no convincing that hard times were ahead. After observing the voting in November 1867 for the constitutional convention, he noted that "all the trash & negroes voted the radical ticket...what we are coming to, time will tell. Nothing good I fear." The Republicans carried almost every county and elected all but thirteen of the 120 convention delegates. When it assembled in Raleigh in January, the convention drafted the most democratic constitution North Carolina had ever known. It guaranteed manhood suffrage, eliminated property qualifications for state office, provided for the popular election of judges, and replaced the old county courts controlled by local elites with popularly elected commissioners. Gwyn was so discouraged over his future prospects that he planned to do little more with his plantation than "make enough to live on." He expected nothing but "a *great* deal of harm" to come out of the convention. "The South is ruined indeed *I* think," he concluded.

The elite's gloomy view of the future came close to being a self-fulfilling prophecy. Men such as Gwyn had no intention of promoting economic recovery as long as the Republicans were in power and in a position to claim credit for it. After Holden was elected the state's first Republican governor in the spring of 1868, a united conservative bloc of former Whig Unionists and Democratic secessionists did all in their power to undermine the Republican administration. With most of the state's newspapers, landed wealth, and educated class arrayed against them, the Republicans made little headway in righting an economy reeling under wartime losses, crop failures in 1866 and 1867, and a severe shortage of investment capital.

As economic conditions remained dismal, Walter's decision to go into debt to buy his brother's land increasingly seemed like a reckless gamble. His friends cautioned him to prepare for the worst. "The demand for real estate is now so little," noted Walter Steele, "that I fear you will find it to turn out not so well as you have been led to believe. A debt now makes me tremble, and you may find that you have taken upon yourself a load which will be quite cumbersome to you." Isaac Lenoir, a cousin from Sweetwater, Tennessee, pointed out that settlers could purchase land comparable to Walter's at lower prices from the government or in the Tennessee mountains. Feeling that Walter would never be able to repay his debts "under the negro government which will weigh upon us of the South for years," he proposed that Walter seek a release from his contract to purchase all of William's estate. For William Bingham, Walter's plans for his lands would have to be put on hold "till the negro incubus is removed." In a fantasy common to many whites after the war, Bingham argued that African

Americans would not be able to survive in freedom and would die off. "The negro is doomed," he wrote Walter in early 1868, "and unless a merciful Providence interferes, I don't see how a war of the races is to be avoided." Once the deadening weight of the black presence was finally removed, he foresaw a wave of new settlement and capital that would bring about "the glowing future" that Walter had predicted.

During the winter at Crab Orchard sales remained at a trickle, primarily because money was "very scarce." Walter blamed the latest credit squeeze on the sharp drop in cotton prices in 1867 that had depressed markets in the Lower South for bacon and livestock, the chief sources of cash for mountain farmers. He was discouraged but determined not to give the Yankees the satisfaction of admitting failure: "I must stand it, & I think that I can do so as long as the Yankees can." As for his vows during the war to leave the South before submitting to Yankee rule, he now conceded that "Brazil & other comparatively stable & free honestly conducted governments are too far off for an old man to hop to on one leg."

Walter left Crab Orchard in the fall of 1868 to resume his surveying in Watauga and to begin laying out town lots at Hickory Tavern in Catawba County. His 565 acres there lay within a mile of a railroad depot and, he believed, were easily worth $5,500 if sold in a single block. Knowing that no buyers would step forward at that price, he decided to lay off lots on each side of a broad avenue and donate alternate lots "to persons who would improve them respectably." He would also enhance the moral character of what he envisioned as a growing commercial center by donating at least ten acres to any religious denomination or philanthropic organization that would build a college or high school. Moreover, as he noted to James Gwyn, "if such a thing could be started, it would greatly enhance the value of the land."

In Watauga, Walter set aside for the family a large tract of land along the Boone Fork that he deemed too valuable to be sold at the current depressed prices. Since he could not afford with his pressing debts to carry this land himself, he offered it as an investment to his brother-in-law James Gwyn. He also tried to interest Gwyn in a tract of the Beech Creek lands that possibly contained valuable deposits of silver. A prospective buyer had backed out of a sale, and Walter was desperate to reduce his debts. Although reluctant to divert capital from his mercantile business and skeptical from the start of Walter's land venture, Gwyn felt an obligation to assist his wife's brother. He agreed to reduce Walter's debt to him by $2,000 in exchange for the Beech Creek property. With even greater reluctance, Rufus agreed to buy 400 acres that adjoined the Boone Fork tract of 1,000 acres in Watauga that Walter, after Gwyn's refusal, now hoped his sister Sarah would take as payment for the $3,000 he owed her. For himself, Walter reserved a tract of land at the head of the Linville Gorge, a parcel that struck him as richer than the Boone Fork tract and "exceedingly beautiful in its scenery." It was here that he planned to retire.

By the summer of 1868, Walter was resigned to realizing little from his land sales "for a long time." However, he still believed that they would be "lively when radicalism is once thoroughly defeated." In the meantime, he began preparing for a permanent move to Watauga that would place him closer than Haywood to his main landholdings. He still had a lot of surveying to finish, and he had to be physically present to show the land and draw up contracts for purchasers and renters. He expected to spend the next two winters at Crab Orchard looking after his cattle and sheep and would then move his livestock to Watauga once his new home was ready.

Walter and his friends fared better in the first year of Republican rule than they had expected. To be sure, no economic recovery was in sight, but conditions had stabilized. After two abysmal years, the harvest was good, and despite dire warnings in the conservative press of racial violence and Republican schemes to confiscate land, the wealthy were left undisturbed in their property holdings and the freedmen peacefully signed labor contracts. From Orange County in the central Piedmont, William Bingham reported that "the general impression in these parts is that we have touched bottom" and that the freedmen were "quiet & do but little stealing." Having had no problems with his black hands at Crab Orchard, Walter pretty much agreed. He had been temporarily shaken by the news of a minor race riot in Asheville on the day of the presidential election in November 1868. A mob of young white males went on a rampage after a freedman protested being denied the right to vote by a white election clerk. The mob shot and killed one African American and injured eighteen others. Walter, and nearly all other whites, blamed the disturbance on the blacks and felt they had received a well-deserved lesson. He assured James Gwyn in December that "the negroes here are very quiet & orderly since their riot at the election." He was even happier to note that "their number here is said to be diminishing, the mortality among them being very great." Then, in a bitter swipe at Republican efforts to annex the Dominican Republic, he added, "What does the president want with St. Domingo? To bury them in?"

These African Americans registering to vote in Asheville in 1867 eagerly took part in a political revolution that stamped Reconstruction as unacceptably radical for most Southern whites.
(SOURCE: Harper's Weekly, *September 28, 1867.*)

In 1869 conservatives counterattacked in a well-coordinated campaign against the Republicans. Taxes, traditionally very low in North Carolina, had increased sharply under the Republicans, in large measure to fund new social programs such as public education for both races. Conservatives successfully accused Republicans of reckless fiscal extravagance. Exploiting the weakest link in the Republican coalition—the biracial alliance of the rural poor—they appealed to white pride and called for the restoration of white supremacy. To hasten that restoration and demoralize Republicans, respected local conservatives used the Ku Klux Klan and other paramilitary groups to intimidate blacks into submission. Charging that the Republican program of state-supported railroads was riddled with corruption, conservatives forced the state to default on some of its railroad bonds. The Republicans had been guilty of just enough dishonesty and incompetence for the charges of corruption to stick.

The state's mounting fiscal problems came as no surprise to Walter. He had always viewed the Republican leaders as greedy thieves, indistinguishable from the corrupt political rings he believed set policy in Washington. By the winter of 1869 he was expecting that the state would soon have to repudiate its railroad bonds, and he derived a perverse satisfaction from the prospect. What would trigger a default, or as he put it in a letter to James Gwyn in February 1869, "the big vomit of repudiation [which] relieves the stomach of the body politic," would be the political backlash that set in when the Republicans tried to cover the deficit in the state treasury by raising taxes to an "intolerable" level. At that point the Republicans would repudiate the state's debt and find support for such an irresponsible act from "the landless laboring classes, the simple dupes whom they are now leading by the nose," who would eagerly free themselves from the burden of taxation. To survive "the pretty hard struggle to come," the Lenoirs and their friends must "prepare to live in the simplest manner, to be industrious & economical, to work without trying to make all we can, & to be strictly frugal in all our expenditures."

Walter gave Gwyn the same advice he had been giving his family since the end of the war. Rufus did his best to follow it but still found himself squeezed by rising taxes and declining income from his plantation. When he received his bill for county taxes in August 1869, he was short of the funds to pay it. "There is less money & more taxes than I ever heard of before," he wrote Tom. "I see no chance to pay such taxes by farming."

Rufus eventually came up with the money, but many white farmers did not. Sinking ever deeper into debt, some fled their creditors and headed west, with Texas being a favorite destination. Others with more substantial property holdings migrated out of fear that their property would not be secure once the Republicans assumed control of the county governments. In a panicky tone, Bingham informed Walter in the summer of 1869 that "radicalism is prevailing generally in our township elections, and bringing on its inevitable consequences. Property in the region is growing more insecure, and violence is taking the place of law." A rash of barn burnings, presumably by angry black tenants who had been evicted, brought out the Ku Klux Klan, and Bingham was concerned that mob law was about to be imposed. Still, he could not condemn the vigilantes: "Property must be protected, and it is simply impossible to do this with carpet-bag judges and legislators elected by negroes." Unwilling to accept the rule of those they deemed incapable of governing responsibly, many of Bingham's wealthier neighbors pulled up stakes and left in the fall of 1869. They were among "our best people," he told Walter, and they were so anxious to get out that they sold their personal property "at great sacrifice" and left with their lands unsold.

For Walter the news from Bingham confirmed that the South had "reached the philosophical stage of drowning which comes on after the struggle is over." He resolved to take no interest in the disgusting spectacle "except as matter of polite curiosity." Instead he would stick to his self-imposed hardship and isolation for however many years it took to settle his land matters "so that they would be in no danger of breaking any one else down." In the fall of 1869 he explained to Archie Christian, his brother-in-law in Virginia, that he could not break free to pay him a visit because "I have no hopes of escaping for several years to come at least, from the confining business which now occupies me. But the dream is too pleasant & I am of too hopeful a disposition to abandon it entirely."

Walter was working himself to exhaustion in pursuit of his dream. In addition to traveling to remote sites for field surveys, arranging meetings with prospective buyers, and attending court to file land papers, he was spending his winters working at Crab Orchard. Too tired to read or write after his evening meal, he retired for a few hours of fitful sleep only to work half the night at his desk. He knew he was stretched too thin but refused to slow down. Part of what drove him, he told Gwyn, was his conviction that it was "a blessed thing for a Southern gentleman in these days of our political degradation to be worked hard all the time, especially if he can work with any reasonable hope of making both ends meet in a business point of view." Having lost political power at the hands of the Yankees, self-respecting Southern whites were honor bound to establish a record of business success.

In the winter of 1870, Walter and Tom completed surveying their lands in Haywood. Between them they owned over 10,000 acres, and the growing problem of trespassers left them anxious to record an airtight title to it. One of the trespassers, in Walter's eyes at least, was Thomas Crawford, a tenant of his for fifteen years. Crawford had claimed a right of possession to sixty acres of Walter's Crab Orchard property and refused to leave. After bringing suit in Superior Court, Walter backed off and accepted the loss of what he deemed as "not very valuable" land. In addition to his other work that winter, he contracted with a builder for a house and mill on his property at Shulls Mill in Watauga.

Walter finished surveying his land in Watauga in the summer of 1870 and made a promising start on a settlement there. But he soon realized that his ambitious building plans called for more cash than the sale of his lands could provide, and "the money does not come in fast enough to pay my current expenses." Reluctantly he concluded that he would have to sell his Haywood lands. Not only did he need money, but his land business required his presence in Watauga nearly year-round. He first offered his Haywood property to Gwyn, who expressed no interest. So he listed the holdings with the North Carolina Land Company for a year with instructions to sell it for a minimum of $5,750. He still hoped to retain for the family what he referred to as "the cream of my Watauga lands," the 1,200-acre tract along the Boone Fork he had set aside for Sarah that adjoined land Rufus had already purchased from Walter. However, Rufus felt he had overpaid Walter for his land, and Sarah made no business decisions without Rufus's approval, so nothing was done, leaving Walter angry and hurt.

As Walter was exploring options to raise cash and reduce his debt, the Republican administration under Governor Holden was fighting for its survival in the wake of an upsurge in Klan terrorism in the spring of 1870. The troubles climaxed with the killing of two prominent Republican politicians in Alamance and Caswell counties. Formerly reluctant to act, Holden now sent white militia units raised in the western counties into Alamance and Caswell. Under the command of George W. Kirk, the Union officer notorious for his wartime raids into western North Carolina, the troops arrested about 100 men, including some of Holden's most outspoken political critics. Bypassing the local courts, which were controlled by the Klan, Holden ordered the suspects tried before a military commission. He was forced to turn them over to Federal authorities when outraged Democrats jumped on his highhanded tactics and obtained writs for their release under the Fourteenth Amendment and the Habeas Corpus Act of 1867, legislation intended to protect the rights of the very blacks and white Unionists the Klan had been terrorizing. Raising the cry of endangered white liberties, the Democrats carried both houses of the state legislature in the August elections and impeached Holden the following February.

Despite their legislative victory in 1870, the Democrats were forced to share power with the Republicans for the next six years. The issues of reform and equal rights championed by the Republicans still won the support of the poorer voters of both races. Even after Holden's ouster, the Republicans had enough strength to vote down a Democratic-sponsored attempt in 1871 to call another constitutional convention and to carry the elections for president and governor in 1872. Meanwhile, the Democrats remained in firm control of the legislature.

For Walter and other white conservatives, the Democrats' partial comeback was no panacea. Republicans continued to dominate many county governments where they set policies on schools and tax rates and adjudicated most legal disputes. William Bingham was hoping for a Democratic victory in the presidential election of 1872 if no other reason than to free the South from protective tariffs and "New England monopolies." He expected the radicals to triumph, however, for "radicalism is omnipotent in America, & it is manipulated by the money power, which is in the hands of the monopolists." The Republicans, he predicted, would spread enough lies about the Ku Klux Klan "to blind the

North to the oppression the poor are suffering for the benefit of the rich."

Walter's financial situation grew increasingly desperate. On into the 1870s, there were few takers for his lands in Watauga. The only person offering to buy was one Henry Moore, an African American. Inquiring whether Walter would sell to a "negro," Walter's land agent hastened to note that "Henry is a very good Negro and minds his own business and he can pay you fore it." Walter went ahead with the sale. Rather than buying land from Walter, whites in Watauga were more intent on poaching his timber. Sales of land were little better in Hickory Tavern. Despite a pickup in the summer of 1871, Walter soon admitted to Tom that "the growth of the place so far is not substantial and under bad management."

In the fall of 1871, still anxious to sell his Haywood lands, Walter subdivided some of them to market to local buyers. He felt good about his prospects "of selling them to good neighbors and at much better prices in proportion to their real value than I could get for my Hickory tavern & Linville lands." But by the spring, Walter realized that he had miscalculated: no one would buy his Haywood lands for cash. He was in "a death struggle," he told his niece Laura; "I can only sell land on a credit and can get no money on the notes. I have to compound the interest of the notes that I owe, and do not see how I can raise money any longer to pay taxes." The corrupt Republican "army of tax gathers" was draining the South of its productive wealth and destroying all forms of enterprise save for "official stealing." Had it not been for those taxes, Walter was certain that the postwar Southern economy would have prospered with an infusion of emigrants and outside capital. The mountains of North Carolina, he insisted, were "certainly by nature one of the most valuable and desirable portions of the U.S." and "radical misrule" had prevented honest men from making a decent living and impoverished all those who had debts to pay.

Out of money in the spring of 1872, Walter focused entirely on his land sales. However, he had put too much work into improving his stock farm at Crab Orchard to abandon it completely. Instead, he arranged with Jesse Anderson, the tenant with whom he had boarded since the war, to feed his livestock in the winter after they were brought down from the summer pastures. Anderson would also maintain the hay meadows and monitor the work of the other tenants.

Walter had additional plans at Crab Orchard to build stables, a workshop for his tools, shelters for his wagons and lumber, a springhouse, and an apple house for storing the fruit from his maturing young orchards. But none of the proposed purchasers for his Haywood lands were able to raise funds for the required down payment. Lacking the funds to finish what he had begun at Crab Orchard, he turned over management of his beloved farm to Anderson.

Walter fully grasped his predicament. "I am rich enough to feel how poor I am," he told Gwyn, "rich enough in land to be very poor till I get rid of it or have the means to improve it." The solution to his dilemma seemed simple enough: sell most of the land, clear his debts, and improve one piece with the proceeds from the sale of the remainder. But that was just what he had been trying to do for the past five years. Even after giving up hope of finding cash buyers for large tracts, he was unable to sell small tracts on long-term credit to meet his expenses. Most of his purchasers had been landless poor whites anxious to secure a homestead for their families. Few could afford to put any cash down, and many had fallen behind in their credit payments. Still, as Walter emphasized to Gwyn, "no other class of persons seem now to care to buy lands," and money was so scarce that offering his land at a third of his asking price would likely not attract many new buyers. As long as his delinquent families were working hard to enhance the value of their land, Walter was willing to be indulgent with them. Indeed, improving mountain lands had always been one of his main goals. Had he been out of debt, he would have been satisfied with his sales to date.

His debts, however, continued to rise. A speculative bubble in railroad securities broke in 1873, setting off shock waves in financial markets that triggered a national depression. Prices for the South's major agricultural commodities plunged and the region's already inadequate credit supply tightened up even further. Only Gwyn's timely assistance kept Walter out of bankruptcy. After first assuring Walter that he was content with interest-only payments on what Walter owed him, he in effect cancelled the entire debt when he agreed in 1873 to purchase the Haywood lands that Walter had been unable to sell. Relieved of that large debt and free of the expenses he had been incurring at Crab Orchard, Walter was able to survive the long depression that persisted until 1878, but just barely.

He closed the gap between expenses and income by selling his lands piecemeal, as needed. Whenever he had any surplus cash, he plowed it back into his land in the form of improvements. The surpluses, however, were few and far between. As he confessed to

Rufus, "I can barely live & make a few scratches towards preparing my land for nephews & nieces who have none of it in the wild state I will leave it in when I die. The fault will be in them, not in the land." Or rather, he added, the fault should rest with the government which "so burdens us with debt & mad extravagance that it is no longer easy to live by farming."

Walter's lament over the future of farmers was a common one in North Carolina by the 1870s. The recovery of the agricultural economy from wartime losses had been, at best, slow and halting, and Walter's nephews were among the many sons of the prewar farmers and planters who had no intention of following in the footsteps of their parents. All James Norwood, Joe and Laura's son, wanted to do was "to make my escape while I am young." "Things at home look gloomy," he wrote Walter in 1875. "Parents growing old and feeble—going down into old age in debt and poverty and the sisters growing old with so little to make life happy and desirable and I too poor to help them any and wanting to marry a delicate girl." After saving some money working for his cousins in Tennessee, Norwood planned on heading to Texas where he hoped to find "enough rich land to make me independent." Walter Gwyn, Walter's namesake and James's son, opened a law practice in Asheville where he handled some of Walter's land business. Gwyn Lenoir, Rufus's eldest son, left home as a teenager. Although Rufus was disappointed, he understood his son's decision. After all, he noted, Gwyn was obliged to see farming as "a slow business the way we manage it—Not much good stock—behind in farming utensils—lands not improving—no money making—*No mules to sell*—seasons too short for cotton—& too dry for grass."

Like Rufus, Walter understood the reluctance of the sons in the Lenoir clan to go into farming in their native state. Whatever they did, he urged them to avoid the entrapment of debt and to live like free men. "He who doesn't pay his way as he goes is some body's pauper [and] will end in having the soul of a slave," he counseled Wat (Walter) Gwyn, while he who pays his own way is "the freest of the free." Of course Walter was speaking from bitter experience. For over a decade, he had felt smothered by debts that in his mind reduced him to the abject dependency of the slaves who had always served for whites as a frightful model of what not to become. To free himself of this sense of defilement, he would continue to accept whatever hardships he would have to endure to regain his financial independence.

At least the election results of 1876 brought some satisfaction. A campaign to restore white supremacy returned conservative Democrats to power in North Carolina. They ran up large majorities in the legislature, elected the popular wartime leader Zebulon Vance as governor, and won popular approval of amendments proposed by a constitutional convention of 1875 dominated by the Democrats. The most important of these amendments put power back into the hands of local elites by granting the legislature control over county governments. Elsewhere in the former Confederate South, the remnants of Radical rule collapsed when the Republicans bargained for Southern support in order to secure the presidency for Rutherford B. Hayes in the aftermath of the disputed Hayes-Tilden election.

James Norwood expressed the joy of most Southern whites when he exclaimed to Walter in December that he was as "happy as ever a shouting Methodist was at camp meeting—& tho I now believe that Hayes will be inaugurated, I believe that we have a *solid* South, & that the time is now at hand that the place of the carpet-bagger will know no more for ever." Concerned that Southern honor was once again being impugned by reports in the Northern press that hotheaded Southerners would resort to violence to prevent an electoral vote in favor of Hayes, Walter felt compelled to write to a Northern editor setting the record straight. Adopting a magnanimous tone befitting an honorable Southern gentleman and Confederate veteran, he offered assurances that the South would peacefully accept Hayes's election. No one in the South wanted more bloodshed, he insisted, least of all former Confederate soldiers.

Contrary to the expectations of many whites, the overthrow of Reconstruction did not produce an immediate economic upturn in North Carolina or elsewhere in the South. That would have to await the end of the national depression in the late 1870s and the willingness of Northerners by the 1880s to invest in a South they finally deemed to be politically stable. When the economy did pick up, those who benefited the most were manufacturers, town developers, and farmers who made a successful transition to the new cash crop of tobacco. Crop prices, however, continued to fall and small farmers sank deeper in debt. What prosperity there was largely bypassed rural areas.

The flow of capital into manufacturing and towns that could tap into an expanding network of railroads produced the first sizable sales that Walter realized from his Hickory Tavern properties. "Hickory (incorporated as a city in 1870) is growing more rapidly than ever before in population and business," he happily informed Rufus in the winter of 1880. The new growth industry of tobacco was key. The light, sandy soils on the piney ridges across the Carolina piedmont, considered almost worthless before the war, were ideally suited for the bright-leaf variety of tobacco used in the manufacture of cigarettes, a relatively new product aggressively promoted after the war by North Carolina entrepreneurs like James Duke. Two large tobacco warehouses had recently opened in Hickory, and five tobacco factories were slated to begin operations soon.

Walter used the income from the sale of his lots in Hickory to pay the interest on his debts and finance his milling business close to his new home in Shulls Mill in Watauga, but the money went out as fast as it came in. In building a new dam for his gristmill in 1881, he had been forced to tear down his old sawmill and now had no money to pay for a new one. He pleaded with his contractor, C. J. Cilley, to build the mill on credit. He explained that he could expect no help from any of his other debtors and described himself as "a beggar" in "trying to build a mill & conquer a small stock farm from the Watauga forests in order that I might make my own living, I have worked hard, lived hard, worn rags, & banished myself from society, &, perhaps in my case harder still, from my books." Won over by this heartfelt argument, Cilley built the mill.

Relieved that he had survived what he called his "time of greatest need," Walter was decidedly more cheerful when he wrote his niece Laura Gwyn that fall with news of all that he hoped to accomplish. He was starting two grass farms for his cattle and sheep and was expanding his milling business at Shulls Mill, but most of all he was looking forward to the day when he could retire at Linville. His favorite spot there lay at the foot of

Grandfather Mountain, the highest peak in the Blue Ridge range. He referred to it as Under the Pinnacle and pronounced it "one of the loveliest places in all the mountains." "I am in love with it," he told Laura, "& want, when I can get it sufficiently improved, to make my home on it." He found the site all the more appealing because the South Atlantic & Ohio Railroad was about to reach Cranberry, just twelve miles away. The coming of the railroad, he predicted, would open up the scenic wonders of Watauga to out-side visitors and promote the economic development he had long wished to see. In his mind none of this would have been possible under Republican rule. As he put it to Laura, "Truly we are mak-ing wonderful progress at the South since we have escaped from the grip of the carpetbaggers."

In the winter of 1882–1883 Walter cut his remaining ties to Haywood. His brother Tom died in January, having struggled con-stantly to make a living after the war. Like most Southern farm-ers, he never had enough money. What he did earn he insisted on using to pay off his debts even though he was able to collect little from his debtors. As his farm languished and his wife Liz-zie suffered from chronic poor health, he took pride in honoring his obligations, including paying a $4,000 debt for some slaves bought just before the war. It took more than ten years to clear the debt, but in doing so he felt "more like a free man than if I had withheld what justly belonged to [his creditors]." Two weeks after Tom's death, Walter Gwyn reported from Asheville that he had found a buyer for Walter's last tract of land in Haywood.

An article that appeared in the Raleigh *News and Observer* in the spring of 1882 so upset Walter that for the first time in his life he ran for political office. The article named Walter as one of a number of prominent North Carolinians who had recently "embraced the knees of the President [the Republican Chester A. Arthur] and besought his smiles on their efforts to obtain office." Walter denounced the charge as "slanderous" with a card (or printed announcement) in the local press. As an honorable Southerner, he protested, he had always shunned the Republicans and "their high crimes against the life of liberty." Like many true Southerners, he had fought the war, he declared, "to defend a few abstract doctrines of States rights against the usurpations of the Federal government." Unlike some former patriots, he would never shame his native land by seeking office at the hands of a party committed only to the "mad and revolutionary exercise of power." He warned that if the Republicans succeeded in luring enough Democrats to restore the popular election of county officials, the eastern counties with large black populations would elect corrupt and incompetent governments. Economic paralysis would once again grip the state. He chided the *News and Observer* for even thinking that he would cooperate with the Republicans. His honor was at stake.

Walter's family name and his stature as a war hero ensured a wide reading for his card. Encouraged by a show of public support and still anxious to vindicate his name, he announced his candidacy for the legislature as a representative from Watauga. Easily elected, he went to Raleigh in December to serve in the legislative session of 1882–1883. Like many Southern Democrats representing upcountry farming districts, Walter defended the interests of debt-ridden farmers who wanted relief from tight money and scarce credit in more flexible money that was not tied to a gold standard. For these farmers, the tyranny of the Federal government after the war had taken the form of revenue agents whose efforts to collect a national tax on whiskey provoked a violent response in mountain districts where backwoods distilleries were a source of both profit and pleasure. Walter saw himself as the farmers' spokesman when he introduced resolutions in January 1883 that called for an end to the Internal Revenue Service, a reduction in the protective tariff, and greater economy in the Federal government.

Although flattered when the legislature voted to send his resolutions on to North Carolina's congressional delegation, Walter had no intention of seeking a career in politics. Reporting to his sister Sarah from Raleigh in February 1883, he indicated that after having "hid away so long in my semi-hermitage among the wild mountains," he doubted whether he would be able to match wits, "as warriors of old were wont to measure swords," with the state's "most accomplished sons." He had worked hard, shunned no responsibility, and was astonished to note that he had been "listened to with greater attention in the august presence of the House of Representatives, than when I was trying to talk to the little gatherings of my constituents in Watauga." With a sense of pride in a job well done, he was ready "to gladly retire at the end of the session."

Walter left Raleigh in the spring with a cold and a bad case of indigestion and was complaining a year later that his health had not yet fully recovered. Ignoring the advice of friends and family, he continued to push himself with a grueling routine of work. "I find my business here badly in need of me as might have been expected," he wrote Rufus from Shulls Mill upon his return in late March. Terrible weather took a toll on his health. "I have been a close prisoner this winter, walled in by snow & ice, rain & mud," he wrote Rufus in March 1884. "I never took so little exercise for so long a time together, when able to go; & that, & care about my affairs has made me more puny than usual." He was especially frustrated at not being able to walk on the ice or snow without falling. During the periodic thaws, he had to stop frequently to pull his "wooden leg, sometimes with the aid of both hands, from deep mud." He felt that his health and strength improved when he was able to work outside and "stump around" after his farm hands, but he had to admit that "the symptoms of old age seem to be growing me rapidly on me of late." What most lifted his spirits that winter was a report in the newspaper that explained the bad weather and the strange atmospheric conditions at Shulls Mill that produced a veil around the sun and incredibly vivid red sunsets. They were part of the global fallout from the momentous volcanic explosion that blew up most of the island of Krakatoa near Java on August 23, 1883.

Never permitting himself a break from self-imposed burdens, Walter suffered a mild stroke the following August. Still weak ten days after the attack, he asked Sarah to come out and look after him for a while. All he remembered was that he had felt dizzy when his vision blurred with a "glimmer before my eyes" and he suddenly fell and sprained his hip. Adding to his problems that fall was a cash squeeze that forced him to borrow another $300 to get through the year. Interpreting his stroke as a warning that he was running out of time to settle his scattered land business, he wrote his debtors in early 1885 that he was prepared to sue them if they did not make a good-faith effort to repay at least part of what they owed him. Wat Gwyn, whose

Western Carolina Land Agency was now providing Walter with legal advice and promotional services for his land business, was able to collect $400 from two debtors that spring. Enough trickled in from his other debtors to alleviate the worst of his cash problems.

Walter's family reacted to his brush with death by redoubling efforts to convince him that he had to join a church to have any hope for eternal salvation. Walter thanked his niece Mary Ann for her concern over his "spiritual welfare" and confessed that he could give her "no *good* reason" why he was not a member of the Reformed Episcopal Church of his parents and other family members. He certainly felt an affinity for their creed and often thought of joining but had habitually hung back. As to why, he could only repeat what he had often told his mother: "My strongest hindrance, I will not call it reason & you need not tell me that it is utterly illogical & inconsistent if presented as a reason, is my sense of utter personal unworthiness, which helps to reconcile me here to a life on the outskirts of society." Unworthy in his mind of fellowship either with God or human society, he continued in his self-inflicted banishment.

When Mary Ann urged her brother in the spring of 1885 to come to Green Hill and recuperate under her care, Walter answered that "I am in the tread mill, & I do not know when I can get out of it long enough for such a visit." He needed a long rest, but he refused to take it out of fear that any time away from his land business would result in the sacrifice of all that he had worked so long to achieve. Sensing that he had little time left, he pushed himself even harder. Although reading and writing became difficult as his eyesight began to fail, he still spent countless hours keeping up with his business correspondence, copying and ordering the field notes of his various land surveys, and poring over numerous newspapers. As he raced against the clock to finish all he had dreamed of accomplishing, the death notices in the newspapers left him feeling even lonelier. As he reflected in a letter to James Gwyn in 1885, "How fast they are departing this summer who belong to the generation who were mostly youths with you, & those a little younger with me. The fast recurring news of their departure makes me feel more lonesome here, even here in my remote Watauga solitude."

The only release he found from his work was in his dreams. He grew closer to his nieces in his declining years and shared with them his reveries of escape from the burdens that exhausted him. One dream transported him to the warmth of Florida, where he could spend his winters under the watchful eye of a good physician and nurses. Another lifted him above the frozen ruts and the deep mud and slush that were so treacherous for his wooden leg, to soar through the sky with the flocks of pigeons he never tired of watching from his home in Shulls Mill. How much he enjoyed tracing the daily flight of the pigeons as they departed at dawn from their roost on the Blue Ridge in Surry on their way to "an early breakfast" in Caldwell and Burke—and then seeing them return at sunset "in swift flight back after supper to that same distant roost." As he watched "this wonderful phenomenon, morn & eve, day after day," he found himself "dreaming that human angels might yet do the same."

The dream that kept him tied to his work was, of course, his plans for his land and his visions of what western North Carolina might become. Although it took longer than he ever imagined, that dream began to approach reality in the 1880s when the completion of long delayed railroad projects opened up the region to tourists and outside investors. Walter first noticed a change in 1885 with the opening of the Watauga Hotel at Blowing Rock. For Walter, the hotel's instant success as a fashionable summer resort heralded an end to the county's isolation and the beginning of sustained growth. He could barely contain his enthusiasm when he wrote James Gwyn that Watauga would soon be "spoken of as a favored land, destined ere long to become a delightful region, the home of wealth & culture & progress. Behold the realization of my idyl!"

Lumbering also expanded in the mountain counties with the coming of the railroad as Northern concerns were drawn to the region's magnificent hardwoods. A company headed by the Smart brothers of Boston approached Walter in 1885 with an offer to mill the lumber on some of his tracts. Walter granted them an option until the end of the year to purchase both the trees and the land that he owned in Linville, but the Smart brothers were unable to follow through on their offer.

Walter now considered selling only his cherry trees, his most valuable timber, at $6 per 1,000 feet. He estimated that he had about a million feet of cherry and would realize close to $6,000 from the sale. Before he found a buyer for the cherry trees, however, Samuel T. Kelsey, a developer of resort properties in western North Carolina, offered to buy 8,090 acres of Walter's lands in Linville and on Grandfather Mountain for $28,000. The offer was a godsend. Kelsey agreed to pay $10,000 down and had up to eight years to pay the remainder. To preserve the scenic beauty of the site, Walter stipulated in the agreement that the head

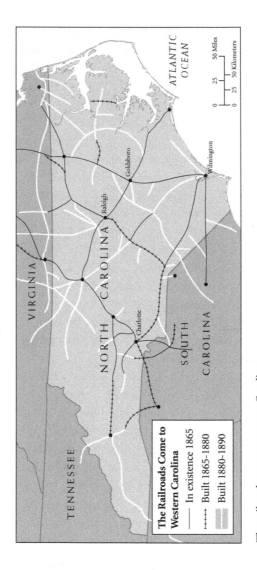

The railroads come to western Carolina.
Especially by the 1880s, new rail lines opened up the mountain counties to tourists and businessmen.

By the 1880s railroads were carrying tourists to new resort hotels in the mountains of western North Carolina.
(SOURCE: *North Carolina Collection, Pack Memorial Public Library, Asheville, North Carolina.*)

springs of the Linville River, as well as the springs and streams on the side of Grandfather Mountain that flow into the Linville, "shall be protected and secured from contamination in future." Additional conservation safeguards called for the preservation of a "broad belt of timber" on the side of the mountain and the setting aside "forever" of a free public access to the highest peaks of the mountain by a carriage road and foot and bridle paths. But Kelsey lacked the clout to follow through on his plans, and

Golfers prepare to tee off on the course of the Hot Springs Hotel northwest of Asheville.
(Source: *North Carolina Collection, Pack Memorial Public Library, Asheville, North Carolina.*)

in 1888 he sold his option to Hugh McRae, an industrialist and developer.

Walter viewed his sale as yet another sign that the South was finally achieving the economic progress he had envisioned for it once slavery ended. One of Rufus's sons, another namesake by the name of Walter, had left home and was working at odd jobs in California and Texas. When he sought his uncle's advice in the fall of 1887 on whether he should seek his fortune in Argentina, Walter replied that his prospects would be brighter in his native South. Sounding like a booster, Walter touted the "Sunny South" as having a better climate, population, and government than any country in South America and credited its rapid economic development for "fast making it the richest country in the world." Stay in the South, he advised, and become a carpenter or brick mason in one of our mushrooming cities. He had no doubt that "fortunes were awaiting builders all over the South"—builders like Hugh McRae.

Paradoxically, the pending sale resulted in Walter working harder than ever, to prepare the deed and mortgage and convey payment title in fee simple for all of the parcels of land. In addition to the ongoing demands of collecting rent from his tenants and attending to his milling and livestock at Shulls Mill, he now had the time-consuming chore of combing through and organizing his field notes for the thousands of acres involved in the Linville sale. Despite feeling tired all the time, he refused to take the rest he so desperately needed.

To the surprise of no one in his family, he suffered a second stroke in May 1889, which left him partially paralyzed on his left side. He was weak but in no pain and this time also he almost welcomed the sense of calm that overcame him. "I was not afraid then to die," he wrote Rufus, "almost wanted to die as I lay there so calm & free from pain, feeling that I was taking a good rest from which I did not want to be disturbed." Although he had no fear of death, he wanted to keep living because he still had so much to do: "I want very much to get my papers & property arranged so that they will be less trouble to the family when I am dead, & the sale of my Linville lands will soon put me out of debt & in easy circumstances, & enable me to realize some of the good results of my patience in holding on so long to my apparently unprofitable lands."

After making out his will on May 30, 1889, naming Tommie Lenoir, one of Rufus's sons, as his executor, he recuperated for six weeks at Fort Defiance. Attended by a nurse, he was back at Shulls Mill in the summer of 1889. Ignoring the pleas of his sister Mary Ann to "just let it go!" he immersed himself in his Linville papers. Hampered by his difficulty in writing legibly and his inability to read more than four hours a day, his progress was agonizingly slow. He had no illusions that he would ever regain his health. Still, he no regrets and he refused to complain. Rather, as he wrote his niece Laura Gwyn, he chose to accept his afflictions as the will of his "loving heavenly Father" whose just chastisements had made him "an humbler & a better man." Now, finally, he felt worthy enough to accept baptism in his parents' church.

The onset of cold weather drove him first to a room at an inn in Hickory and then over to Fort Defiance in March 1890. On Easter Day, April 6, he joined the Protestant Episcopal Church. When Rufus's son Tommie accompanied him back to Shulls Mill in June, Walter was still rushing to finalize all the details for a meeting with the directors of McRae's land company on July 16. He was "running on the *midnight* meal schedule once more," as Tommie put it in a letter to his mother, and subsisting primarily on a diet of milk. In late June, at Walter's request, his nieces Selina Norwood and Sallie Gwyn came out to assist Tommie in nursing Walter and to prepare his meals. His spirits picked up with their arrival and his appetite improved. He enjoyed their company, especially their daily readings of the Bible in the morning and evening. The next two weeks were the happiest he had experienced in years.

The meeting in July with McRae's associates went fine and Selina recalled that Walter was "cheerful & bright" when they returned on July 17. At long last, it seemed clear that the venture would be successful—a "crown of glory" to his old age, as Wat Gwyn had put it, which would handsomely benefit the seven family heirs in his will.

Four days later, Walter suddenly changed his daily routine. As Selina recalled, everything Walter did that day was out of the ordinary. After insisting on accompanying Tommie to the post office at Blowing Rock on a raw, damp morning, he returned around noon and for the first time ate a meal outside his room. He laughed and joked through the meal and entered a mock protest when his nieces reminded him that he should follow his doctor's orders and avoid certain foods. Upon finishing the meal, he sent Tommie off on an errand to pay some field hands about four miles away, a trip that would take most of the afternoon. As Tommie was about to leave, Walter called him back and "tenderly took his hand and told him good bye." Tommie was surprised, for he expected to see Walter again in a few hours. Then it was Selina and Sallie's turn to be surprised. For the first time, Walter did not ask them to sit down with him and read from the Bible. Instead, he asked to remain alone in his room. After placing a bell next to him so that he could ring for assistance, his nieces were struck by the "tender loving tone" with which he thanked them. When a neighbor dropped by with a request for honey, Selina and Sallie knocked on Walter's door, saying that they needed the key to the storeroom. After asking them who the neighbor was, Walter fell silent. Rather than disturbing him, his nieces returned to their sewing. They soon heard noises: he had moved into the lounge. Increasingly concerned by Walter's strange behavior, Selina waited about a half hour and then called to him. No answer. When she

Shown here in 1904, Rufus outlived all his Lenoir siblings.
(SOURCE: *North Carolina Collection, Wilson Library, University of North Carolina–Chapel Hill.*)

looked in, she "saw in an instant that he was stricken, never to rise again." His only response when she begged him to speak was a trembling of his lips.

He was carried to his bed, where he remained unconscious for the next five days as friends and family stayed at his side. Rufus and his wife arrived the day after Walter's attack, and Hugh McRae and Samuel Kelsey came over from Linville. Walter was aware of their presence. His eyes teared when Selina spoke to him, and he slowly rubbed his fingers over her palm.

When Walter seemingly decided on that July Monday to welcome the long rest he had for so long denied himself, it was the middle of summer, his favorite season in the mountains he so loved. It was then, as he once wrote to a niece, that "Watauga dons her summer costume [and becomes] the fairest of the daughters of the land of the sky." His troubled soul had always found solace in the beauty of the mountains, and it was only fitting that he departed when that beauty was at its loveliest. He died the evening of July 26, 1890. As he wished, he was buried in the family cemetery at Fort Defiance next to his wife Nealy and infant daughter Anna. In his heart, he had never left them.

NOTES

For the framing of the Fourteenth Amendment and the struggle between President Johnson and Congress for control of Reconstruction policy, see W. R. Brock, *An American Crisis: Congress and Reconstruction, 1865–1867* (New York: Harper Torchbook, 1966). Eric Foner, *Reconstruction: America's Unfinished Revolution, 1863–1877* (New York: Harper & Row, 1988) is a comprehensive, modern treatment of Reconstruction as a whole, but no comparable study exists for North Carolina. Although still useful, J. G. de Roulhac Hamilton, *Reconstruction in North Carolina* (New York: Columbia University Press, 1914) is marred by its racist assumptions and anti-Republican bias and should be offset with Otto H. Olsen, "North Carolina: An Incongruous Presence," in *Reconstruction and Redemption in the South* (Baton Rouge: Louisiana State University Press, 1980) and the firsthand account presented in Albion W. Tourgeé, *A Fool's Errand: A Novel of the South during Reconstruction,* ed. George M. Frederickson (New York: Harper & Row, 1961). The rise and fall of the Republican party in the mountain South is covered in Gordon B. McKinney, *Southern Mountain Republicans, 1865–1900: Politics and the Appalachian Community* (Knoxville: University of Tennessee Press, 1978).

On the formative role of African Americans in Reconstruction, see W.E.B. Du Bois, *Black Reconstruction in America, 1860–1880* (New York: World 1935); and Steven Hahn, *A Nation under Our Feet: Black Political Struggles in the Rural South, from Slavery to the Great Migration* (Cambridge: Belknap Press, 2003). Violence, especially against black activists, played a larger role in overturning Reconstruction than Walter ever acknowledged. Allen W. Trelease, *Klan White Terror: The Ku Klux Conspiracy and Southern Reconstruction* (New York: Harper & Row, 1971); and George C. Rable, *But There Was No Peace: The Role of Violence in the Politics of Reconstruction* (Athens: University of Georgia Press, 1984) tell the story of white terrorism and include much material on North Carolina.

The economic problems of the South after the war, which doomed Walter's efforts to quickly sell off the land he had gone into debt to purchase, are covered in Roger L. Ransom and Richard Sutch, *One Kind of Freedom: The Economic Consequences of Emancipation,* 2nd ed. (New York: Cambridge University Press, 2001); and Gavin Wright, *Old South, New South: Revolutions in the Southern Economy since the Civil War* (New York: Basic Books, 1986). C. Vann Woodward's classic *Origins of the New South, 1877–1913* (Baton Rouge: Louisiana State University Press, 1951) offers the best analysis of the new political economy that emerged in the South after the end of Reconstruction.

Economic conditions in western North Carolina and the coming of industrialization are treated in Ronald D. Eller, *Miners, Millhands, and Mountaineers: Industrialization of the Appalachian South, 1880–1930* (Knoxville: University of Tennessee Press, 1982). On the railroads that served as an agent of change and opened up more of Walter's land to timber interests and tourists, see Edward L. Ayers, *The Promise of the New South: Life after Reconstruction* (New York: Oxford University Press, 1992). For the rise of the tourism that would bring Walter's economic salvation, see Richard D. Starnes, *Creating the Land of the Sky: Tourism and Society in Western North Carolina* (Tuscaloosa: University of Alabama Press, 2005).

One of the delights in research is the unexpected discovery. After I had given up hope of learning much about the circumstances of Walter's death, I was going through the James Gwyn papers in the Southern Historical Collection, a wonderful source for the evocative letters that Walter wrote his nieces as his health was declining in the 1880s. There I found Selina Louisa Norwood's letter of July 31, 1890, to her Aunt Mary Gwyn that detailed Walter's unusual activities on the day of his fatal stroke.

Afterword

—∿∿—

I FIRST BECAME AWARE OF WALTER LENOIR SEVERAL YEARS AGO when I was selecting some of the Lenoir family's wartime correspondence for a posting on a university website on the Southern home front during the Civil War. His remarkable letter of July 1863, arguing that Southern whites had nothing to fear from emancipation because the Union army would exert tight control over the freed slaves and never allow them to retaliate against their former masters, gave a fresh insight into how Southern whites reconciled themselves to the collapse of slavery. It indicated, even as the war continued to rage, the underlying conservatism that informed Northerners' approach to both emancipation and the eventual place of African Americans in American society.

Realizing that Walter was exceptional in the clarity and directness of his thinking, I explored further and ran across a letter describing his moral misgivings about slavery. This was the letter of April 1858 in which Walter announced that he and his wife Nealy had vowed never to own another slave because of the "evil of being a master and mistress of slaves." When I then discovered that Walter was set to move to the North in 1860, I was hooked. I became fascinated by what I saw as the central question posed by his life: why did a politically conservative Southerner personally opposed to slavery who had decided to leave the slave South for the free North commit himself heart and soul to the Confederacy when the Civil War broke out?

As I learned more about his war experiences, it became apparent that much of what he did and thought would remain a mystery unless I could understand why his decision to support the Confederacy in 1861 was irrevocable; why he withdrew from Southern society after his devastating wound in 1862; why he lived as a virtual hermit in the isolation of the mountains of western North Carolina. In short, my core question quickly produced a host of others. My unfolding research soon convinced me that any adequate telling of Walter's story could do it justice only by seeing it as a whole in which each part created a context for what was to follow. In turn, a biographical approach required showing how Walter's life opened a window onto the larger narrative of nineteenth-century Southern history and the questions that historians and the public have raised about that narrative.

Much of my enjoyment in working on Walter's story came in seeing how it added depth and nuance to what I thought I knew about the nineteenth-century South. Since my graduate days in the 1960s, I had inclined to the view that Southern whites closed ranks when confronted with the abolitionist movement in the 1830s and, aside from a few brave individuals, defended slavery as a positive good, an argument that received its classic treatment in Clement Eaton's *The Freedom-of-Thought Struggle in the Old South*.[1] However, my research showed that virtually none of the

Lenoirs or their friends had a good word to say about slavery. Almost uniformly, they described owning slaves as a burden. They tried to take seriously what they saw as their obligations as Christian patriarchs to provide for the spiritual and material welfare of their slaves and foster their domestic relations by keeping families together. Working land that was declining in fertility, they grumbled incessantly about how the costs of retaining so many slaves condemned them to agricultural practices that yielded little in the way of a sustained return. After all, their Carolina lands lay well north of the prime cotton and sugar districts of the Lower South. Most of all, the Lenoirs described how uncomfortable they felt when they had to punish individual slaves to induce obedience in the others.

At the same time, they had no intention of relieving themselves of their self-imposed burden by selling off their slave property. They depended on slave labor for the material comforts they enjoyed, and their position as slave owners bestowed a power and status they accepted as their just due. When market conditions were favorable and they needed the money, they cast aside their paternalism and sold off individual slaves, even at the cost of separating children from their mothers. In short, they were willing to benefit economically from an institution of human bondage they recognized as morally questionable. They made the all too convenient trade-off in their minds of viewing slavery as both wrong and necessary. In addition, the strict manumission laws across the South made it more difficult for individual masters to free slaves. Those who did so had to provide for moving any freed slaves out of state.

The extensive role of tenancy in the agricultural operations of the Lenoirs before the war was another surprise in the research.

Until recently, historians and economists viewed widespread farm tenancy in the South as a post–Civil War development, a product of the upheaval of emancipation and Reconstruction. New research has revised that view by revealing high rates of tenancy among white farmers in the 1850s, especially in the upcountry and in areas with the worst lands for producing staple crops.[2] By then tenant farmers and other landless laborers made up a third or more of the free households in the Southern rural economy. In the mountain counties of western North Carolina that Walter came to know so well, up to 40 percent of the whites who worked on the land did so as tenants or day laborers. Wealthy families like the Lenoirs bought up huge amounts of raw acreage at low prices and then designed entrepreneurial strategies that depended on renters and hired hands to work and improve that land for eventual sale. By so doing, they were able to manage and profit from vast, scattered tracts of land while concentrating their limited family and slave labor on their home plantations. The economic and social transactions that flowed from these labor arrangements created webs of mutual dependence in rural communities otherwise divided by immense disparities in wealth and power.

The way the Lenoirs and their poorer neighbors in Caldwell and Haywood counties responded to the secession crisis demonstrated that, as persuasively argued by Daniel W. Crofts in *Reluctant Confederates*, Lincoln's election did not immediately unify the slaveholding states in support of secession.[3] Indeed, the four northernmost of these states—Delaware, Maryland, Kentucky, and Missouri—never seceded from the Union, though the Confederacy claimed the latter two. North Carolina, joined by Virginia, Tennessee, and Arkansas, was among the middle tier of states that left the Union only when Lincoln called for troops to suppress the Confederacy. Far from uniting Southern whites against the perceived threat posed by Lincoln's election, the push for secession led by South Carolina produced dangerous signs of polarization within the region. As the letters between Walter and Zebulon Vance suggest, a majority of whites outside the cotton states of the Lower South denounced secession as reckless and incomprehensible. They predicted that efforts to leave the Union would lead to a civil war and the end of slavery—the institution that secessionists were so anxious to defend. Rather than rushing to join the Confederacy, they rallied behind Unionists in hopes of working out a compromise that could peacefully restore the Union.

Unionists in the Upper South benefited from an organizational base of support unavailable to the cowed and outflanked moderates in the Lower South. Whereas two-party competition had withered in the cotton states in the 1850s as states' rights Democrats exploited the slavery issue to build up large majorities, it continued to flourish in the Upper South, where the level of slaveholding and the proportion of slaves in the population were roughly half those in the Lower South. Slavery was relatively less important in the Upper South because the region lacked the soil and climate for the large-scale production of rice, sugar, and cotton, the slave-produced cash crops that were the mainstay of the plantation economy. Selling slaves to the Lower South, where demand remained high, enabled planters in the Upper South to finance a program of agricultural diversification and manufacturing in which free labor was gradually making inroads at the expense of slavery. The result was a range of social interests and competing views on economic development that found expression in the ongoing competition

between Democrats and Whigs. As long as this competition persisted, voters in the Upper South had an alternative to the extreme Southern rights' stance of the Democratic party when it came to protecting their individual liberties.

Whigs in the Upper South, including established planter families like the Lenoirs, overwhelmingly opposed immediate secession. As long as the incoming Lincoln administration made no aggressive move against slavery or any state that had seceded, they saw no need to leave the Union. The Republicans, they stressed, did not control Congress or the Supreme Court and would have to pursue moderate policies if they hoped to win the presidency again in 1864. While conceding that the Republicans presented a grave threat to slavery, they insisted that the South had ample means of protecting the institution within the Union. The very worst policy for the South would be to follow the lead of conspiratorial plotters who would sacrifice the interests and safety of the South to satisfy their political ambitions. Fleeing the Union for a new political confederation would only plunge the nation into the horrors of a civil war.

The Whigs provided the community leadership and the organized party support that blocked secession in the Upper South during the winter of 1860–1861. Joining this Unionist coalition were many Democratic nonslaveholding farmers from the uplands and mountains. As was true across the South, areas with high concentrations of slave ownership voted for John C. Breckinridge, the presidential candidate of the Southern Democrats in 1860. These voters were most likely to favor immediate secession. But the slaveholders' push for secession in the Upper South nearly backfired on them. The Unionist majority was made up of businessmen and slaveholding Whigs, who depended on continued economic cooperation with the North, and nonslaveholders who resented efforts of the "slaveocracy" to railroad them out of the Union. If these interest groups coalesced into a new and permanent political party, Democrats wedded to plantation agriculture faced a very uncertain future. They would be shut out of power in their own states at the same time that the secession of the cotton states had sharply undercut the ability of these planters to defend their interests in the Federal government. The idea of a middle confederacy, which Walter favored, was still under consideration in early April 1861 and a conference of the border states was scheduled to meet in late May at Frankfort, Kentucky, to deliberate on the issue.

The nation was at war by the time the Frankfort conference met. The Unionist coalition in the Upper South had shattered in an instant when Lincoln responded to the firing on Fort Sumter with his call for troops. Suddenly the secessionists in the Upper South, some of whom were ready to attempt a forcible seizure of power in their states, found themselves in an overwhelming majority. Like the Lenoirs, virtually all white families in the Upper South had kin and friends scattered across the Confederacy, and they rejected out of hand waging a war against their own flesh and blood. Like Walter, they were caught up in a wave of emotion that committed them to the Confederacy with a degree of unity that was inconceivable before war broke out. And because they saw Lincoln's proclamation as a declaration of war against all they held dear, they were able to convince themselves that they were fighting to defend not primarily slavery but their liberty as a free people.

As James Gwyn was so quick to note, not all Southern whites rushed to show support for the Confederacy as troops mobilized in the spring of 1861. Dissent was so pervasive in the western mountain counties of Virginia that the Union was able to detach the region from the Confederacy and admit it as the new state of West Virginia in 1863. East Tennessee might have split off as well if it had not been so inaccessible to Federal forces. In North Carolina, dissent became a serious political problem by 1863, and Walter echoed the charge of most Confederates when he identified internal opposition to the war as a more serious threat to Confederate success than advancing Union armies.

The extent to which divisions on the home front contributed to Confederate defeat has been a lively topic of historical debate since the appearance in 1986 of *Why the South Lost the Civil War*. That work argued for the shallowness of Southern nationalism as the decisive factor in that defeat.[4] The contrasting positions taken by Gary W. Gallagher's *The Confederate War* and William W. Freehling's *The South vs. the South* offer a good introduction to the current debate.[5] Whereas Gallagher stresses that most Southern whites remained unshaken in their allegiance to the Confederacy and argues that defeat can best be explained by military reversals, Freehling insists that the 450,000 troops raised by the Union in the slave states—close to 150,000 black soldiers and sailors and 300,000 white soldiers, 100,000 of whom came out of the Confederate states—gave the Union cause an advantage that Confederate armies could not overcome. For Freehling, the Confederacy collapsed from within as significant numbers of Southerners defected to the Union.

As the wartime experiences of the Lenoirs and other North Carolinians reveal, evidence can be marshaled on both sides of this debate. Walter was the only Lenoir brother who made a total commitment to fighting in the Confederate army until sidelined by his wound. After serving out his twelve-month volunteer enlistment, Tom returned home and limited his involvement for the remainder of the war to leading scouting parties searching for deserters. Rufus sat out the entire war and never seemed to have a significant emotional investment in the Confederacy. Still, Tom and Rufus remained loyal Confederates. The same was true for most members of the elite, who backed the Confederacy mainly because they had so much to lose in a Union victory. Open defiance of the Confederacy was largely limited to the lower classes, those whom the Lenoirs described as the uneducated and the ill-bred. It emerged in the first year of the war and grew steadily. By the fall of 1864, Zebulon Vance concluded that "the great popular heart is not now, and never has been in this war."[6]

At the root of the disaffection was a growing perception that the conflict was, in the phrase of the day, "a rich man's war and a poor man's fight." In order to wage a long war, the Confederate government centralized its power to draft men and economic resources, a course that struck many as tyrannical interference with their persons and property. As the war dragged on, growing numbers of dissenters accused the Confederate government of the very tyranny and centralized despotism they had originally identified with Lincoln's government. Worse yet, Confederate policies seemed to favor the rich at the expense of the poor. Nothing symbolized this unfairness more in the eyes of common whites than the so-called Twenty Negro law of October

1862 that granted draft exemptions for overseers on plantations with at least twenty slaves. The wealthy were also far more likely to receive draft exemptions for service in local militia units. The policy of conscription was always open to the charge of class bias because it fell heaviest on nonslaveholding families whose economic survival depended on the labor of husbands and teenage sons. By the same token, the impressment of slaves and other property was an inconvenience to planters, but the loss of a draft animal or farm equipment could spell ruin for a yeoman farmer. Rising taxes, impressment, unrelenting inflation, destructive military raids, and a shortage of family labor pushed many nonslaveholders into poverty. No wonder that, as Tom Norwood wrote in the spring of 1864 of the soldiers in the North Carolina 37th, many of his rank-and-file soldiers questioned whether they had any "primary interest" in a war that demanded so much and was seemingly fought to benefit the wealthy and protect their slave property.

For all the discontent that culminated in what can best be characterized as an inner war in many parts of the state, North Carolina contributed men and resources to the Confederacy to the very end. Indeed, no Confederate state proportionately contributed more. Comprising only one-ninth of the white population of the Confederate states, North Carolina furnished one-sixth of all Confederate soldiers and recorded an extraordinary one-quarter of all Confederate battlefield deaths. North Carolina and Georgia alone accounted for over 40 percent of all Confederate conscripts east of the Mississippi. Along with two states in the Southeast, North Carolina supplied two-thirds of all the direct taxes raised by the Confederate government.

Vance's leadership as war governor after 1862 accounted for much of this remarkable record of sacrifice. The frantic tone of Walter's letter to Vance in the spring of 1864 on the dangers posed by Holden's peace movement showed how much the elite relied on Vance for keeping North Carolina in the war. Vance did just that while casting himself as the defender of white liberties in his highly publicized disputes with Jefferson Davis over the constitutionality of Confederate measures. His innovative programs of state-subsidized relief helped mitigate the harsh slide of many nonslaveholding families into poverty and enabled him to maintain the popular base of support he needed to draw heavily on the resources of the state for the war.

Vance, however, did not eliminate the stark divisions within North Carolina. They persisted after the war and framed white politics during Reconstruction. After a long period of neglect in which African Americans were caricatured as ignorant pawns or nonparticipants, black Southerners have been brought to center stage in the modern historiography on Reconstruction, especially since 1988 by Eric Foner's masterly study.[7] In danger of being lost, however, in this long needed shift is the perspective of many prominent white families. We cannot understand Southern white culture today without understanding the path that elites took in constructing a sense of the Lost Cause that looms so large even today, long after the end of the war.

For Walter Lenoir and most of his correspondents, disaffected and alienated poor whites were the central actors who would determine the shape and direction of Reconstruction. Upper-class whites assumed that the freed people lacked the capacity for informed or independent political participation. The freedmen represented a political threat only to the extent that poor whites exploited the black vote to create an unholy political alliance intent on confiscating the land of the elite. Even during the war Rufus Lenoir Patterson, Walter's cousin and a wealthy merchant and factory owner, railed against the "low-bred agrarians" who stirred up class resentments: "Every man who is pursuing an honest calling & realizing *profits* is denounced by these people … & they are crying out, 'Oh, for the old Union that Lincoln might confiscate the property of the *rich* and give it to the *loyal* poor.'"[8] Confederate defeat heightened fears among the elite that poor whites and freed blacks would come together in a political majority that would unseat the wealthy from their accustomed positions of power and privilege.

President Andrew Johnson's lenient terms for white Confederates, as well as the pacifying presence of Federal troops, enabled the elite in North Carolina to establish some control over the volatile situation. By 1866, most of the state's wartime leadership was back in power. But in reasserting their control, they steadfastly refused to extend a political voice or the equal protection of the law to Unionists and African Americans. This refusal convinced congressional Republicans of the need for sweeping democratic change, which that the elite equated with the majority rule of an ignorant rabble of blacks and whites. Once Republicans ruled the state in 1868, the wartime divisions took the form of fighting for or against the Republicans. What John Inscoe and Gordon McKinney wrote of politics in the mountain counties held true across the state: "the two parties … recognized that they were just carrying on the internal war of 1861–65 in another guise."[9] Alarm over the confiscation of their property resurfaced among the elites and was quieted only with the ousting of Holden in 1870 and the return of the legislature to Democratic control. The relief deepened in 1876 with Vance's victory in the gubernatorial race and the election of Hayes, a moderate Republican, to the presidency. As James Norwood correctly foresaw, Hayes pursued a policy of reconciliation so that Southern whites would "think that the Republicans are very good fellows after all."[10]

Eight years after Walter's death, conservative whites crushed the remnants of the democratic promise of Reconstruction. Voted into office largely by poor white and black farmers, a fusion ticket of Republicans and Populists gained control of the state government in 1894 and immediately set about to undercut the political and economic power of the postwar elite of planters, industrialists, and businessmen. The elite responded to this threat with a massive white supremacy campaign that in 1898 toppled the Republican government of Wilmington in a vicious coup d'état that signaled a return to the use of fraud and intimidation to cow black voters and drive white farmers out of their alliance with blacks. The Democrats rode that campaign back to power and consolidated their victory by disfranchising black voters. Jim Crow laws soon followed that stigmatized African Americans and granted poor whites the psychological satisfaction of a guaranteed superiority over blacks. The democratic changes dating to Reconstruction had finally been overturned.

The massive unrest and bitterness of the 1890s would have taken Walter by surprise. He spent the last years of his life convinced that the South was in the midst of an economic revival that validated his belief that the end of slavery would usher in a new age of sustained economic progress for the South. That revival was real enough to attract Northern investors to the mountains of North Carolina and set in motion the offer that enabled him to sell the lion's share of his landholdings at a handsome profit to himself and his heirs. The burst of development in the 1880s, however, never benefited most mountain farmers. As the region's population more than doubled between 1860 and 1900, farmers were pressured to divide their farms to leave shares for family members. Farms grew smaller and less productive and mounting debts drove an increasing number of farmers into tenancy or farm labor for others.[11] An economic depression that spread over the nation in 1893 and persisted for the next five years devastated farmers and fueled the agrarian insurgency that the elite smashed in 1898.

Walter failed to see that the prosperity of the 1880s bypassed most North Carolinians—confirmation that his elite perspective remained. His story, like any biography, cannot serve as a stand-in for the history of the time in which he lived. Our sense of North Carolina history in the nineteenth century would be quite different if we related its history from the perspective, say, of Delia, the young slave woman whom Walter so resolutely whipped in November 1864 or of Thomas Crawford, the white tenant who challenged Walter's ownership of some of the land at Crab Orchard in 1868. We write the history of the Walter Lenoirs of North Carolina and elsewhere because the social and economic status of elites leave a large and determining impact on how the past comes to be understood. In addition, wealthy, prominent families like the Lenoirs account for most of the personal correspondence and written records that are essential to the writing of narrative-driven history. Yet their personal accounts of what was happening around them were biased and shaped by their own values and priorities. Rather than explaining historical processes, a biography is far more likely, as Peter Walker has pointed out, to "illustrate history by personality."[12]

For all the limits of the biographical approach, it remains indispensable for uncovering the individual choices that transform abstract historical processes into concrete actions. Slavery produced more than one elite group of Southern whites, and each group confronted the secession crisis with its own experiences and expectations. Walter's story is valuable precisely because his understanding of the slave South and his place in it was quite different from that of the fire-eater elite centered in South Carolina. Elites in the Upper and Lower South were divided over how to react to Lincoln's election. Walter's eventual commitment to the Confederacy reveals how the outbreak of the Civil War reunited the South's ruling classes. Defeat in the war solidified that unity in their common embrace of the Lost Cause. Thus, with full knowledge that Walter's story, like that of any individual, was unique, I decided to relate a history of the nineteenth-century South centered around his own experiences and emotional perspectives. His story, I hoped, could help illuminate the quite different choices made by other Southerners of his generation.

The abundance of manuscript sources made it possible to reconstruct Walter's life with depth and texture. Most of the sources I used came from the Lenoir Family Papers in the Southern Historical Collection at the University of North Carolina at Chapel Hill, the bulk of which were donated to the university in the early twentieth century by Rufus Lenoir. The Thomas Lenoir

Papers of Walter's father at Duke University and the James Gwyn Papers at the University of North Carolina supplemented these manuscripts. The specifics I could glean of Walter's life opened up a window into the emotional conflicts of a regional culture haunted and defined by a racialized system of slavery and a legacy of defeat and poverty after the Civil War. Although this narrative is centered on Walter, it encompasses his immediate family and friends, as well as his wartime comrades, to give the sense of a social world undergoing wrenching change. Introducing alternative viewpoints helped frame Walter's actions and feelings and added complexity to the narrative of a Civil War South too often depicted in the rigid categories of sectional stereotypes. Because Walter's viewpoint was inevitably subjective, I used it to understand how Southern whites established a cultural identity shaped by the emotional dynamics of the war.

I realized early in the project that in order to understand Walter's life and what it might reveal about the culture of the nineteenth-century South, I had to grapple with the central quest of his life—a search for a morally affirmative identity. As noted in chapter 1, establishing an independent identity was an acute task for planters' sons whose fathers were reluctant to surrender the control that made their sons so dependent on them. The problem of identity was regional as well as individual.[13] By midcentury, Southern whites were increasingly hostile and defensive as they confronted mounting Northern attacks on slavery. Defining themselves in opposition to what they perceived Northerners thought of them, they adopted a more and more Southern version of American identity that affirmed the values of a regional culture and its system of human bondage that provoked so much criticism in the North. Carried to its logical conclusion in the secessionist ideology of the Lower South, this defensive posture made it possible to conceive of an independent South that would vindicate slavery and the virtues of a uniquely Southern civilization to the outside world.

Historian Stephen Berry has argued that the love of a woman and the ambition to leave a lasting legacy were the defining hallmarks of what made life worth living for educated white males in the antebellum South.[14] If so, Walter had failed on both counts as he approached middle age. Nealy, the one great love of his life, died two years after their marriage. Never again would Walter experience the spontaneous joy that his time with her had brought. He groped for the words to express his crushing sense of loss, for how could he ever be happy again? As he had written in his diary before his marriage, "the love of a woman has always been the ground work of all my ideas of dreamland happiness."[15]

As for ambition, he had none after Nealy's death. Uncomfortable with the notion of owning a fellow human being, he had no desire to join his father and brothers in the plantation management of slaves. As a student at the University of North Carolina, he had rejected the family role his father had set out for him—an accomplished scholar who would bring distinction and honor to the Lenoir family name. Ever mindful of the sacrifices his parents were making on his behalf, he turned to the law as a means of relieving his father of the burden of supporting him. But for Walter, law was never an end in and of itself, only a means to achieving a measure of economic success that would justify him in marrying and, as he wrote in his diary, "rearing around me by my exertions a prosperous and happy family. I have already banished from my hope all higher ambition."[16] Once that ambition burned out with the death of Nealy and their infant daughter, Walter dealt with his grief by deciding to exile himself from his native South.

The outbreak of the secession crisis forced Walter and countless other Southern whites to decide between competing loyalties and identities that pulled them to and away from the existing Union. For many, probably most, in the Lower South, Lincoln's election was an act of aggression that endangered the safety of slave society and required withdrawal from the Union. Where cotton was not king and profitable market outlets in free states existed, a sense of Southernism did not preclude remaining in a Union that was still valued as a source of pride and security. In rejecting immediate secession, Walter and most whites in the Upper South were also rejecting the vision of the South they saw represented in the emerging Confederacy.

As portrayed explicitly in the speeches and writings of low country planters in South Carolina, this vision defiantly glorified black slavery as the only proper basis for a social order committed to the moral and material progress of whites. In its boldest form, this vision looked to reopen the African slave trade, expand slavery into the Caribbean and Central America, and place political power directly into the hands of slaveholding whites. Even when scaled back by the founders of the Confederate government in the convention at Montgomery, this vision of the South was too unabashedly tied to the defense and perpetuation of slavery to win majority support in the slave states still clinging to the Union. Worse yet, in their precipitous haste and intolerance, the secessionists of the Lower South seemingly would not stop until they had plunged all the states into a bloody and needless civil war. Why, Walter asked in February 1861, "should we take upon ourselves a war in defiance of our wishes, our counsels[,] our policy and our interests, to forward the interests and selfish ambitions of the states which wage it, and which in doing so treat us not as equals, but as dependents?"[17] Why indeed?

Walter's question was answered for him and for most other whites in the Upper South when Lincoln issued his call for troops. For Northerners, Lincoln's action was hardly intemperate. After all, from their perspective the South had just started the war by firing on Fort Sumter. For most Southerners who opposed the Confederacy of the cotton states, however, Lincoln's call was unprovoked aggression against sovereign states. Having convinced themselves that Lincoln had pledged a hands-off policy toward the seceded states in return for ongoing efforts in the Upper South to work out a compromise, they reacted with stunned disbelief. They accused Lincoln of treacherously deceiving them. Never would they wage war against kin and loved ones in the Lower South. Jonathan Worth, a North Carolina Unionist before Lincoln issued his call, wrote, "I am left with no alternative but to fight for or against my section...Lincoln has made us a unit to resist until we repel our invaders or die."[18]

For Southern moderates, Lincoln's call shifted responsibility for war from scheming hotheads in the Lower South to a power-hungry Republican majority in the North. Originally seen as the aggressor, the Confederacy in their minds now became the aggrieved. The Confederacy they pledged allegiance to was not necessarily (and in most cases was not) the nation-state that had come into being at Montgomery, but the local communities they now saw under attack that comprised for most of them the emotional and geographic reality of the world as they experienced it. The result was the distinction between nationalism and patriotism drawn by Robert Bonner in his fine study of the "flag culture" of the Confederacy, a distinction that helps clarify the unresolved debate over how much dissent on the home front contributed to Confederate defeat.[19] Most Confederates, Bonner argues, remained firm patriots in their emotional attachment to a collective war effort against Yankee "aggression," an attachment expressed in the martial sacrifices symbolically represented in the battle flags of Confederate armies. Nationalism, support for political independence as embodied in the Confederate nation-state, was always a more tenuous commitment that Bonner contends never attracted the same primal loyalties and passions. With the surrender of Confederate armies, Southern nationalism died but an abiding sense of Southern patriotism lived on to sustain a belief in Southern whites as a separate and special people in the postwar Union.

Walter's total commitment to the Confederacy as both a patriot and a nationalist marks him as an exception to Bonner's depiction of Southern loyalties. Once he convinced himself that the North was to blame for the war and the South was utterly blameless, he finally found a home in the South, a set of attachments and loyalties that filled the emotional void in his life after Nealy's death. He could no longer love Nealy, but he could love his idealized conception of the Confederacy as the embodiment of all that made life worth living. Like others who volunteered for military service and remained die-hard Confederates, the war and the sacrifices it entailed enabled him to fulfill all the roles that Southern culture demanded of its sons and husbands as defenders of a threatened homeland. In Walter's case, the most elemental role was of a man tough and hardened enough to stand up to the physical and life-threatening demands of war. He constantly emphasized his ability to do so in his letters back home.

Walter so valued his newly acquired martial manhood that the loss of his leg at Second Manassas was a devastating blow to the identity he had created for himself as a soldier. The most common psychological response to the amputation of a limb is anxiety and depression, a sense of loss similar to the grief felt at the death of a loved one such as a spouse.[20] As he had after the loss of Nealy, Walter responded by physically withdrawing from Southern society. To the bafflement and disappointment of his mother and siblings, he retreated to the isolation of the North Carolina mountains and coped with his grief as he eked out a bare existence living alone with his slaves. His loss, however, did not rob him of the soldierly pride he had felt as he bonded with his men in the camaraderie of camp and the heat of combat. Nor did it weaken his support of the war effort or the Confederate government. Unlike those who turned against the Davis administration, Walter had nothing else to lose that he valued. Neither the deteriorating Confederate economy nor the onerous demands of its tax gatherers had much impact on his self-imposed poverty. Nor did he have any worries of being drafted into the army. As for his slaves, he looked forward to the day when he could drive them away. Thus he remained a loyal Confederate to the very end, much like those Southern refugees who had fled from the Yankee invaders and willingly surrendered much, if not all, of their property and personal belongings in the cause of independence. These refugees could still vote, and throughout the war they supported politicians who favored seeing the war through to a successful conclusion.

Unlike Rufus, whose pardon from Johnson arrived in August 1865, Walter never sought a presidential pardon. In his mind he had done nothing wrong and hence would not demean himself by seeking forgiveness. During Reconstruction he continued to denounce Yankees as malignant oppressors who were depriving Southern whites of their right to self-government. He viewed congressional Reconstruction as a bloated monstrosity that combined hypocritical cant about the equal rights of the former slaves with support for the disreputable whites who lusted after the land and property of the true Southerners who had stood by the noble effort of the Confederacy to secure the political and constitutional liberties of whites in the South. Like many Southern whites after the war, he was engaging in the politics of memory.

Memory, as a host of recent studies has shown, is never fixed.[21] Rather than a static remembrance and retrieval of a commonly agreed on set of experiences, memory, both for individuals and for cultures, is an active and selective process of constructing the past as noteworthy for what is forgotten as well as what is chosen to be remembered and celebrated. By creating a memory of the past that forges emotional and political bonds in the present, groups rely on collective memory for sustaining their identity and defining their goals for the future. The need for a collective identity to bind together and define a group is greatest in a time of shared trauma that destroys or radically alters the patterns of life that had sustained old traditions. It is then, wrenched out of the only life they have known, that groups engage in what Eric Hobsbawm has called the "invention of tradition" to create a new group identity.[22] In much the same way as the Cajuns of Louisiana defined themselves in terms of the memory of their expulsion from British Canada in the eighteenth century or African Americans from their shared memory of the horrors and violence of slavery, Southern whites coped with the pain of defeat through a selective remembrance of their past that set them apart as a special and innocent people who had been grievously wronged.

Much was at stake in the effort headed by former Confederate politicians, generals, and ministers to shape and control the social memory of the South. To the South's traditional ruling class, which had led Southern whites into a disastrous war, it surely mattered how the war was remembered. In order to reclaim its influence in sectional and national affairs, this class had to convince Southern whites, and eventually Northerners as well, that the South had fought for a worthy cause and that Confederate leaders had been justified in their actions. Lost Cause advocates gave Southern whites a past of which they could be proud by relating a narrative of Southern innocence and Northern guilt. In this recasting of the past, slavery vanished as a cause of the war, abolitionist meddling was behind all sectional tensions, the prewar South was a golden age of harmony and prosperity for free whites and enslaved blacks, and the Confederacy united all Southerners in a cause of political independence that was all the holier for having been waged against insurmountable odds.

Although Walter was never active in Confederate veterans' organizations or other groups that publicly promulgated the Lost Cause, he found in its romanticized past a way of dealing with his resentment. It was only after the war when the plantation regime lay in ruins that he characterized the old planter class, especially its women, in terms of grace and elegance. As if projecting onto all plantation mistresses his idealized memory of Nealy, he insisted to his sister Sarah in 1866 that nothing better illustrated the superiority of the prewar South than "the contrast between the ladies of the South and of the North.... The lady of Southern society was, in her manner and her character, more simple, graceful, more approachable and affable, yet more dignified and reserved … and she was free from any approach towards a certain masculinity of thought and action which so commonly gives a repulsive hardness to the female character at the north."[23] His use of the past tense was deliberate for he feared that the "true Southern character" would not survive the war. In lamenting its passing, he was castigating the coarse new order he accused the North of fastening on the South. Most striking, Walter erased slavery from his memory of what had brought on the war. During the secession winter he had no doubt that the obsessive fears of planters in the Lower South over the safety and future of slavery in a Union headed by a Republican president were the root cause of reckless efforts to destroy the Union.[24] When he was about to run for public office in 1882, he proclaimed that the war had been fought over "a few abstract doctrines of State rights."[25]

Following the overthrow of Reconstruction, advocates of industrialization and social progress touted the need to build a "New South," whose material abundance would vindicate the congratulatory values of the Old South so glorified in the mythology of the Lost Cause. While promising to unleash a program of economic change that would transform the South with factories and growing cities, these advocates also vowed to uphold the ideals of the Old South by retaining the racial and class hierarchies that promoted the social balance and order essential to moral progress. The success of their program, they argued, would be the surest way of honoring the Confederate war dead. The ideals of the South they had fought and died to defend would live on in a South that would never again be so undeveloped economically as to allow Yankee domination in the future.

Walter's vision of a New South sustained him in the isolation, poverty, and physical misery of the last third of his life. He had never felt at home in a South whose defining institution was slavery. He committed himself to the South and identified himself as a Southerner only when he felt that his native section was unjustly attacked. When the victorious North forced Southern whites to relinquish slavery, he was free to embrace a postwar South that for him was both made noble through its heroic sacrifices and cleansed of the moral impurities of slavery. This was a South he could love. The dreams that had anchored his identity—domestic bliss with Nealy and Confederate independence—had ended in death and defeat, and his "dream," as he put it, of what the South could be without slavery provided the only moral compass he could latch onto after the war. In order to convert his family's vast acreage into a model of development for others to follow, he embarked on the reckless gamble in 1867 of going heavily into debt. He would promote a morally praiseworthy and economically sustainable prosperity in the North

Carolina mountains he adopted as his home. The realization of this dream became the defining mission of his life and the source of his sense of worthiness.

It surely was not a coincidence that Walter deemed himself worthy of receiving God's grace and joining his parents' church only when he was convinced that he was near selling the bulk of his land and realizing a financial windfall for his heirs. In one respect his life remains a great mystery to me. Down to the last few months of his life, he was wracked by a sense of guilt and depravity that I was never able to fathom. Despite a series of personal crises and losses that saw him promise first his mother and then his sister Sarah that he would profess Christianity and turn to God for deliverance, he always held back. Typical of his self-reproach was an entry in his diary penned on the eve of joining the Confederate army. "I am utterly vile," he wrote, "and though I know that God's mercy is sufficient for me I refuse it, and wage a fatal war against myself."[26] Whatever sins he may have committed that so troubled him have been lost to the historical record or, and more likely, were never part of it. Evidently he felt he had atoned for those sins by all the hardships endured in pursuing and then realizing his dream for William's lands. A victim of the pressures of the boom/bust life in the prewar South overlooked in the idealized portrait of the region that developed after the war, William could now rest in peace. His life had not been in vain.

Following his baptism in the spring of 1890, Walter found an inner peace that comforted him as he awaited a death he expected shortly. He died with the assurance of knowing that he had accomplished all that could ever be asked of a dutiful son.

NOTES

1.   Clement Eaton, *The Freedom-of-Thought Struggle in the Old South* (1940; New York: Harper Torchbook, 1964). When it first appeared in 1940, Eaton's study provided groundbreaking documentation of the suppression of free speech in the South in response to the abolitionist crusade.

2.   Frederick A. Bode and Donald E. Ginter, *Farm Tenancy and the Census in Antebellum Georgia* (Athens: University of Georgia Press, 1986) provide the most thorough attempt at uncovering regional patterns of tenancy. Other major studies include Charles C. Bolton, *Poor Whites of the Antebellum South: Tenants and Laborers in Central North Carolina and Northeast Mississippi* (Durham, N.C.: Duke University Press, 1994); and Wilma A. Dunaway, *The First American Frontier: Transition to Capitalism in Southern Appalachia, 1700–1860* (Chapel Hill: University of North Carolina Press, 1996).

3.   Daniel W. Crofts, *Reluctant Confederates: Upper South Unionists in the Secession Crisis* (Chapel Hill: University of North Carolina Press, 1989) focuses on Virginia, North Carolina, and Tennessee.

4.   Richard E. Beringer, Herman Hattaway, Archer Jones, and William N. Still Jr., *Why the South Lost the Civil War* (Athens: University of Georgia Press, 1986).

5.   Gary W. Gallagher, *The Confederate War: How Popular Will, Nationalism, and Military Strategy Could Not Stave Off Defeat* (Cambridge: Harvard University Press, 1997); and William W. Freehling, *The South vs. the South: How Anti-Confederate Southerners Shaped the Course of the Civil War* (New York: Oxford University Press, 2001).

6.   Quoted in Gordon B. McKinney, *Zeb Vance: North Carolina's Civil War Governor and Gilded Age Political Leader* (Chapel Hill: University of North Carolina Press, 2004), p. 234.

7.   Eric Foner, *Reconstruction: America's Unfinished Revolution, 1863–1877* (New York: Harper & Row, 1988).

8.   Quoted in Paul D. Escott, *Many Excellent People: Power and Privilege in North Carolina, 1850–1900* (Chapel Hill: University of North Carolina Press, 1985), pp. 61–62.

9.   John C. Inscoe and Gordon B. McKinney, *The Heart of Confederate Appalachia: Western North Carolina in the Civil War* (Chapel Hill: University of North Carolina Press, 2000).

10. James W. Norwood to Walter W. Lenoir, March 26, 1877, Lenoir Family Papers, Southern Historical Collection, University of North Carolina at Chapel Hill.

11. Inscoe and McKinney, *Heart of Confederate Appalachia*, pp. 266–85, provide an excellent overview of these farmers' economic hardships and the factors behind the "discovery" of Appalachia by outside investors and tourists in the 1880s.

12. Peter Walker, *Moral Choices: Memory, Desire, and Imagination in Nineteenth-Century American Abolition* (Baton Rouge: Louisiana State University Press, 1978), p. xvi.

13. For a probing account of how and why Southerners feel they belong to a different and special culture that sets them apart from the rest of the nation, see James C. Cobb, *Away Down South: A History of Southern Identity* (New York: Oxford University Press, 2005).

14. Stephen W. Berry II, *All That Makes a Man: Love and Ambition in the Civil War South* (New York: Oxford University Press, 2003).

15. Entry of January 18, 1856, in Diary of Walter W. Lenoir, Thomas Lenoir Papers, Duke University Library.

16. Entry of March 3, 1850, Walter W. Lenoir Diary.

17. Walter W. Lenoir to Zebulon B. Vance, February 5, 1861, in *The Papers of Zebulon Baird Vance*, ed. Frontis W. Johnston, vol. 1, *1843–1862* (Raleigh: North Carolina Division of Archives and History, 1963), p. 97.

18. Jonathan Worth to Springs, Oak & Co., May 13, 1861, in *The Correspondence of Jonathan Worth*, ed. J. G. de Roulhac Hamilton (Raleigh: Edwards & Broughton, 1909), 1:143.

19. Robert E. Bonner, *Colors and Blood: Flag Passions of the Confederate South* (Princeton: Princeton University Press, 2002).

20. Colin Murray Parkes, "Psycho-Social Transitions: Comparison between Reactions to Loss of a Limb and Loss of a Spouse," *British Journal of Psychiatry* 127 (1975): 204–10.

21. The most useful of these studies for the refashioning of memory in the postwar South are W. Fitzhugh Brundage, ed., *Where These Memories Grow: History, Memory, and Southern Identity* (Chapel Hill: University of North Carolina Press, 2000); and W. Fitzhugh Brundage, *The Southern Past: A Clash of Race and Memory* (Cambridge: Belknap Press, 2005).

22.   Eric Hobsbawm and Terence Ranger, eds., *The Invention of Tradition* (New York: Cambridge University Press, 1983).

23.   Walter W. Lenoir to Sarah J. Lenoir, January 2, 1866, Lenoir Family Papers.

24.   For the primacy of the slavery issue and related concerns over racial control in the minds of the secessionists, see Charles B. Dew, *Apostles of Disunion: Southern Secession Commissioners and the Causes of the Civil War* (Charlottesville: University Press of Virginia, 2001).

25.   "A Card from W. W. Lenoir," May 20, 1882, copy in James Gwyn Papers, Southern Historical Collection, University of North Carolina at Chapel Hill.

26.   Diary of Walter W. Lenoir, 1839–1861, entry for November 22, 1861.

RECOMMENDATIONS FOR FURTHER READING

---~~~---

NINETEENTH-CENTURY NORTH CAROLINA

Background and Context

Butler, Lindley S., and Alan D. Watson, eds. *The North Carolina Experience*. Chapel Hill: University of North Carolina Press, 1984.

Cecil-Fronsman, Bill. *Common Whites: Class and Culture in Antebellum North Carolina*. Lexington: University Press of Kentucky, 1992.

Censer, Jane Turner. *North Carolina Planters and Their Children, 1800–1860*. Baton Rouge: Louisiana State University Press, 1984.

Crow, Jeffrey, and Larry E. Tise, eds. *Writing North Carolina History*. Chapel Hill: University of North Carolina Press, 1979.

Escott, Paul D. *Many Excellent People: Power and Privilege in North Carolina, 1850–1900*. Chapel Hill: University of North Carolina Press, 1985.

Johnson, Guion Griffis. *Ante-Bellum North Carolina: A Social History*. Chapel Hill: University of North Carolina Press, 1937.

Secession and Civil War

Barrett, John G. *The Civil War in North Carolina*. Chapel Hill: University of North Carolina Press, 1963.

Crawford, Martin. *Ashe County's Civil War: Community and Society in the Appalachian South*. Charlottesville: University Press of Virginia, 2001.

Crofts, Daniel W. *Reluctant Confederates: Upper South Unionists in the Secession Crisis*. Chapel Hill: University of North Carolina Press, 1989.

Inscoe, John C. *Mountain Masters, Slavery, and the Sectional Crisis in Western North Carolina*. Knoxville: University of Tennessee Press, 1989

Inscoe, John C., and Gordon B. McKinney. *The Heart of Confederate Appalachia: Western North Carolina in the Civil War*. Chapel Hill: University of North Carolina Press, 2000.

Kruman, Marc W. *Parties and Politics in North Carolina, 1836–1865*. Baton Rouge: Louisiana State University Press, 1983.

Noe, Kenneth W., and Shannon H. Wilson, eds. *The Civil War in Appalachia: Collected Essays*. Knoxville: University of Tennessee Press, 1997.

Paludan, Phillip Shaw. *Victims: A True Story of the Civil War*. Knoxville: University of Tennessee Press, 1981.

Sitterson, J. Carlye. *The Secession Movement in North Carolina*. Chapel Hill: University of North Carolina Press, 1939.

RECONSTRUCTION

Anderson, Eric. *Race and Politics in North Carolina, 1872–1901: The Black Second*. Baton Rouge: Louisiana State University Press, 1980.

Billings, Dwight B., Jr. *Planters and the Making of a "New South": Class, Politics, and Development in North Carolina, 1865–1900*. Chapel Hill: University of North Carolina Press, 1979.

Harris, William C. *William Woods Holden: Firebrand of North Carolina Politics*. Baton Rouge: Louisiana State University Press, 1987.

McKinney, Gordon B. *Southern Mountain Republicans, 1865–1900: Politics and the Appalachian Community*. Chapel Hill: University of North Carolina Press, 1978.

Zuber, Richard L. *North Carolina during Reconstruction*. Raleigh: Department of Archives and History, 1969.

THEMES IN SOUTHERN HISTORY

Ayers, Edward L. *The Promise of the New South: Life after Reconstruction*. New York: Oxford University Press, 1992.

Bode, Frederick A., and Donald E. Ginter. *Farm Tenancy and the Census in Antebellum Georgia*. Athens: University of Georgia Press, 1986.

Bolton, Charles C. *Poor Whites of the Antebellum South: Tenants and Laborers in Central North Carolina and Northeast Mississippi*. Durham, N.C.: Duke University Press, 1994.

Brundage, W. Fitzhugh, ed. *Where These Memories Grow: History, Memory, and Southern Identity*. Chapel Hill: University of North Carolina Press, 2000.

Cobb, James C. *Away Down South: A History of Southern Identity*. New York: Oxford University Press, 2005.

Dew, Charles B. *Apostles of Disunion: Southern Secession Commissioners and the Causes of the Civil War*. Charlottesville: University Press of Virginia, 2001.

Dunaway, Wilma A. *The First American Frontier: Transition to Capitalism in Southern Appalachia, 1700–1860*. Chapel Hill: University of North Carolina Press, 1996.

Edwards, Laura F. *Scarlett Doesn't Live Here Anymore: Southern Women in the Civil War Era*. Urbana: University of Illinois Press, 2000.

Freehling, William W. *The South vs. the South: How Anti-Confederate Southerners Shaped the Course of the Civil War*. New York: Oxford University Press, 2001.

Gallagher, Gary W., and Alan T. Nolan, eds. *The Myth of the Lost Cause and Civil War History*. Bloomington: Indiana University Press, 2000.

Gaston, Paul M. *The New South Creed: A Study in Southern Mythmaking*. New York: Knopf, 1970.

Gray, Richard. *Writing the South: Ideas of an American Region*. Baton Rouge: Louisiana State University Press, 1997.

Pudup, Mary Beth, Dwight Billings, and Altina L. Waller, eds. *Appalachia in the Making: The Mountain South in the Nineteenth Century*. Chapel Hill: University of North Carolina Press, 1996.

Woodward, C. Vann. *Origins of the New South, 1877–1913*. Baton Rouge: Louisiana State University Press, 1951.

Index

For members of the Lenoir families, see p. xv.

Abolitionism, 41
Abolitionists, 118; linked
    to peace advocates, 122;
    in Lost Cause mythology,
    225
African slave trade, 48–49; drive
    to reopen, 220
Agricultural economy, slow
    recovery of in North Carolina,
    183, 185
Anderson, Joseph R. (Jesse),
    145, 181
Anderson, Josiah, 31
Andy, a slave, 98, 103, 110, 112,
    142, 145
Arthur, Chester A., 188
Asheville race riot, 173
Avery, Mouton, 131
Avery, Waightstill, 19
Avery, William Waight
    still, 131

Ballard, Ann e, 15
Battles: of Atlanta, 133; of
    Cedar Mountain, 77–80;
    of Chancellorsville, 116;
    of Chattanooga, 126; of
    First Manassas, 57, 80; of
    Fredericksburg, 100, 105; of
    Gettysburg, 114–16; of New
    Bern, 63, 71; of Ox Hill, 85–86;
    of Petersburg, 133; of Second
    Manassas, 80–81, 96, 223;
    of Seven Days, 73, 114; of
    Vicksburg, 116–17, 122
Beck, a slave, 98
Berry, Stephen, 219
Bingham, William, 105, 160,
    170–71, 173, 176, 179
Bingham School, 27, 32–33
Black, George, 130
Black suffrage, 167
Blackburn, Jeremiah, 130

Bonner, Robert, 222
Border slave states, 50
Bragg, Braxton, 125–26
Breckinridge, John C., 208
Brownlow, William G., 145–46
Burnside, Ambrose E., 61, 63
Bushwackers, 133, 137–38
Butler, Benjamin F., 70

Caldwell Riflemen, 71
Caldwell Rough and Readys, 69
Calhoun, Andrew, 23
Calhoun, John C., 23
Camp Clingman, 57
Camp Lee, 59–60
Camp Vance, 71–72
Central America, 49, 220
Central Confederacy, proposal
    for, 50, 209
Chancellor, Mrs. Samuel A., 94
Christian, Archie, 176
Christian, Bolivar, 40, 96, 102
Christian, Cornelia (Nealy),
    38–39, 161, 201, 203; death
    of, 40, 219–20, 222
Cilley, C. J., 186
Clay, Henry, 35–36
Confederacy: and Fort Sumter,
    51; as a holy cause, 225;
    centralization of powers in,
    211–12;collapse of, 135,141;
    committed to defense of
    slavery, 220–21; dissent in,
    210–11; formation of, 50;

fulfills Southern cultural roles,
    223; refugees in, 224; turns to
    slave soldiers, 136; wartime
    economy of, 64–65, 68–69, 75,
    104–05, 125
Confederate Conscription Act,
    67–68
Confederate flag, 3–4
Confederate home front,
    unrest within, 56–57, 67, 69,
    114–16, 120, 123–24, 133–34,
    136–38
Constitution of North Carolina:
    amendments to in 1875, 184;
    of 1868, 169; proposals for
    in1866, 157
Copperheads. *See* Northern
    peace party
Cotton, in Confederate economy,
    65–66, 74
Crab Orchard, 127–28, 132,
    139, 142, 145, 171–73, 177,
    182; Walter's love of, 108;
    Walter's plans for, 156,
    161–62, 181
Crawford, Thomas, 177, 216
Crittenden Compromise, 48, 50
Crofts, Daniel W., 206
Cyrus, a slave, 39, 128

Davis, Jefferson, 6, 125, 129, 136,
    213
Delia, a slave, 97, 112, 216;
    whippings of, 98, 132–33

Democratic party, 35; in Lower South, 9, 207–08; in North Carolina, 179, 184, 188, 215
Derr, Jane, 26
Desertion, in Confederate armies, 8, 101, 113, 115–16, 120, 124, 127, 130, 136, 138
Disease, in Confederate camps, 58, 72
Douglas, Stephen A., 41–42
Duke, James, 186
Dula, Thomas, 71–72, 75

East Fork Plantation, 20, 26–27, 29–31
East Tennessee: anti-Confederate sentiment in, 210; deserters in, 101; Republican Radicals in, 158; Union troops and raids, 105, 126, 128, 133, 137
Eaton, Clement, 204
Economy of North Carolina, under Republican rule, 170, 173–76
Elections: of 1860, 41–43; of 1876, 184–85, 215
Emancipation, Southern white attitudes on, 8, 11, 148
England, and Confederate rams, 124–25
Equal rights for blacks, opposed by Southern whites, 145, 147, 157, 167, 214
Erwin, a slave, 29–30, 134

Farthing, A. C., 168
Farthing, Thomas, 120
Faulkner, William, 3, 4
Financial crashes: of 1837, 23, 35; of 1873, 182
Foner, Eric, 213
Foreign-born whites, as labor source in postwar South, 151
Fort Defiance, 16, 20–21, 24, 26–27, 39–40, 158; description of, 14–15; use of slaves at, 25, 38, 144; Walter recuperates at, 198
Fort Pickens, 51
Fort Sumter, crisis over, 10, 51, 209, 221
Fourteenth Amendment, 158, 160, 162, 179; denounced by Walter, 157; rejected in South, 167
Freedmen; and labor contracts, 143, 152, 154–55, 173; and political rights, 147, 157, 160, 167; disfranchisement of, 215; in Southern politics, 169, 176, 213–15; targeted by Klan, 174, 179
Freehling, William W., 8, 210
Fugitive Slave Act of 1850, 47

Gallagher, Gary W., 210
Garrett, Lizzie. *See* Lenoir, Lizzie
George, a slave, 152, 161
Grandfather Mountain: conservation agreements at, 195; Walter's land at, 187, 193

Grant, Ulysses S., 130
Gwyn, James, 21, 56, 68, 115, 162–63, 172, 178, 210; alarmed by Hoke's harsh tactics, 124; and acceptance of Confederate paper money, 113–14; experiments with postwar labor,154–55; laments hard times, 169; on robber bands, 134; purchases Walter's Haywood lands, 182; reaction to Radical Reconstruction, 168; sells slaves during the War, 104
Gwyn, Julia, 115–16
Gwyn, Laura, 186, 198
Gwyn, Mary Ann. *See* Lenoir, Mary Ann
Gwyn, Mary Ann (Walter's niece), 191
Gwyn, Nathan, 70
Gwyn, Sallie, 198–99
Gwyn, Walter, 183–84, 187, 190, 199

Habeas Corpus Act of 1867, 179
Hampton, Wade, 4
Hargrove, Augustus, 29
Harper, George, 73
Hayes, Rutherford B., 184–85, 215
Haywood Highlanders, 54–55, 57–58

Hickory Tavern, town lots of Walter at, 171–72, 180, 185–86
Hobsbawm, Eric, 225
Hoke, Robert F., 124
Holdaway, Rufus, 93
Holden, William W., 158; and peace movement in North Carolina, 120–21, 130–31; as republican governor, 170, 178–79; serves as provisional governor, 145, 215
Home Guard, 123

Impressment, by Confederate authorities, 112, 115, 128–29, 212
Inscoe, John, 214
Isaac, a slave, 30

Jackson, Andrew, 35
Jackson, Thomas J. "Stonewall," 6, 77, 80, 85, 116, 161
Jamaica, emancipation of slaves in, 119
Johnson, Andrew, 145–46, 157–58, 160, 214, 224
Johnston, Joseph E., 141
Judy, a slave, 103

Kelsey, Samuel T., 193, 195, 200
Key, David M., 146
Key, Lizzie, 153–54

Kirk, George W., 135, 178
Ku Klux Klan, 174, 176, 178

Labor, in postwar South, 142–44, 151–55, 159
Lark, a slave, 104
Lee, Robert E., 6, 85, 115–16, 141
Lenoir, Ann, 19
Lenoir, Anna Tate, 39–40, 201
Lenoir, Gwyn, 183
Lenoir, Isaac, 170
Lenoir, Israel, 38
Lenoir, Laura, 21, 32, 35, 53–55, 72, 128
Lenoir, Lizzie, 54, 102, 105, 127, 136, 141, 187
Lenoir, Martha, 19
Lenoir, Mary, 21
Lenoir, Mary Ann, 21, 115, 191, 198; desire to be rid of freed slaves, 148
Lenoir, Rufus T., 52, 59, 74–75, 94, 101, 132, 155, 161, 163; and postwar labor, 152; as a money lender, 43; concern over rural poor, 42; criticized for lack of patriotism, 67; dealings with slaves, 97–99, 103–04, 134; desires no more slaves, 66; economic struggles after the war, 147, 175–76, 183; encampment of Confederate soldiers at Fort Defiance, 128–29; gloomy view of war, 61–63, 66–68, 117, 121; pardoned by Johnson, 224; purchases land from Walter, 172, 178; sits out war, 11, 55–56, 211; slaves of flee to Tennessee, 137; turns back from mission to Walter, 99; wartime taxes of, 113; youth of, 32–33

Lenoir, Sallie, 46, 152–53
Lenoir, Sarah J., 19
Lenoir, Sarah J. (Walter's sister), 21, 32, 70, 127, 129, 152–53, 161–63, 178; urges Walter to return, 155–56
Lenoir, Selina L., 21, 76, 97–98; death of, 131–32
Lenoir, Thomas, 19–21, 24; paternalistic self-image of, 25, 37–38; resented by tenants, 31–32
Lenoir, Thomas I., 35, 98, 112, 127, 133, 138, 177; and local robberies, 134; as a plantation manager, 28–32; barters in wartime economy, 104–05; brings Walter home, 99; cotton speculation of, 74–75, 148; death of, 187; denounces emancipation, 149; depressed after the war, 147–48; hunts for deserters, 101, 113; indecisive as a youth, 26–27; postwar labor arrangements of, 143; raided by Union cavalry, 141; raises a volunteer

company, 11, 54–55; war service of, 57–59, 61, 63–64, 67, 211

Lenoir, Tommie, 197–99

Lenoir, Walter, 196

Lenoir, Walter R., 20

Lenoir, Walter W.: advice on postwar labor, 144, 152–53; amputation of right knee, 91– 93; and sale of slaves, 38, 103–04; anxious to see combat, 64, 76, 82; assumes huge debt to buy out William's heirs, 163–65, 227; commitment to Confederacy, 9–11, 52, 161, 209, 211, 217, 222–23; concedes he cannot emigrate, 171; concerned over an alliance of poor whites and freed blacks, 147, 159, 214; confident in slaves' loyalty during the war, 60; conflicted over owning slaves, 7, 14, 39, 142, 149–50, 203– 04, 219, 227; convalescence in Middleburg, 93– 97; death of, 199–201; debts and poverty of after the war, 172, 177–84, 186, 190–91, 223, 227; declining health of, 189– 91, 197–98; defends his honor, 188; denounces peace movement, 122, 130, 210, 213; dependence on slaves at Crab Orchard, 110–12, 127, 132; desire to uplift landless whites, 164; disdain for his slaves,

127–28, 132, 145; drives off his former slaves, 142; faith in Confederate victory, 70–71, 76, 105–06,117, 119, 120, 125, 138; fears of land confiscation, 146, 158–59, 214; forges a new identity in the war, 8, 96–97, 100, 103,132, 223–24, 227; grief over wife's death, 40, 219; hatred of Union soldiers, 61–62, 122, 131, 138–39; ignores pleas to return home, 132, 155–56; in secession crisis, 43, 47–52, 220–21; land sale to Hugh McRae, 196–99; legal career of, 35–37, 219–20; links black equality with miscegenation,159, 162; love of nature, 134, 156, 192, 200–01; marriage of, 38; on Yankee raids, 126; offers assurances on election of 1876, 185; optimistic over Southern progress, 187, 193,196–97; 215–16; political career of, 187– 89; postwar labor arrangements of, 173; postwar political views of, 156–60, 162, 180– 81, 188, 224; postwar romanticization of Old South, 150, 226; pre-combat war experience, 59–61, 63–64, 68–72, 75–76; prewar political views of, 36, 42; proclaims righteousness of Confederate cause, 57, 62, 80, 95, 116–17, 149–50; racial attitudes of, 144, 159, 162, 173; raided by Union cavalry, 141; recasts his memory of the war, 110, 149–50, 188, 224, 226; rejects living under Yankee rule, 66–67, 122–23, 132; religious views of, 38, 40, 59, 61–63, 76, 86, 88, 95–96, 100–01, 121, 123, 191, 198, 228; response to Union use of black troops, 117–18; returns home and quickly leaves for Haywood County, 100, 103, 106; reveries of escape, 192; romanticized view of women, 37, 161, 219, 226; sees combat at Cedar Mountain and Second Manassas, 77–82; sense of unworthiness, 191, 228; shift in thinking on emancipation, 118–19, 203; stresses postwar need for frugality, 175, 184; struggles as a land promoter, 167–72, 176–82, 185–87, 191–93, 195–98; student at University of North Carolina, 34–35, 219; tries to settle William's debts, 53; trips to the North, 35, 40–41; turns down a military judgeship, 126; use of a wooden leg, 101–02, 106, 112, 168, 190, 192; views of immigrants, 41, 151; vision

for western North Carolina, 192–93; vision of postwar South, 141–42, 144–45, 150–51, 215–16, 226–28; visit to battlefields near Richmond, 72–73; wants to move to the North, 39–41, 150, 204, 220; wartime advice to Rufus, 64–67, 74, 121, 134; welcomes end of slavery, 144, 215–16, 223, 227; wounded at Ox Hill, 85–86, 88–90; youth of, 32–35

Lenoir, William, 14, 37; as patriarch, 19–21, 24–25; career of, 15–19

Lenoir, William A., 27, 37–38; debts of, 23–24, 53; depressed by secession, 52; desire to help landless whites, 164; estate of, 65, 103–04, 133, 163–64; mood swings of, 21–22, 24, 26, 43, 55; on rural poor, 43; speculative schemes of, 22–23, 26; suicide of, 11, 53, 164

Lenoir, William B., 19–21, 38

Lenoir family: as patriarchs, 31, 42–43, 205; and postwar labor arrangements, 151–52; cash dealings with slaves, 103; commit to Confederacy, 209; marriage alliances of, 19, 21; oppose immediate secession, 46, 208; views on slavery, 22, 25, 37, 205; Whig political views of, 35–36. *See also* White tenants

Lincoln, Abraham, 47, 77, 120, 214; and Emancipation Proclamation, 117, 122; call for troops by, 10, 51, 149, 207, 209, 221; election of, 42–43, 46, 206, 220; reelection in 1864, 133. *See also* Fort Sumter, crisis over

Linville: and Walter's retirement plans, 186–87; conservation agreements at, 195; Walter's land at, 172, 193, 197

Longstreet, James, 128–29

Lost Cause, 4–6, 13, 213, 217; and recasting of the past, 225–27

Lower (Cotton) South, compared to Upper South, 7–8, 207–08. *See also* Secession

Manumission laws, 205

Maria, a slave, 98, 110, 112, 127

Mary, a slave, 143

McClellan, George B., 73

McKinney, Gordon, 214

McRae, Hugh, 196–97, 200

Memory, as a selective process, 224–25

Methodist Episcopal Church, 158

Mexican War, 27

Mexico, 49

Middle Confederacy. *See* Central Confederacy, proposal for

Montgomery, Samuel, 102

Moore, Henry, 180

Mountain farmers, growing indebtedness of, 216

New South, and fulfillment of Southern ideals, 226–27

Nonslaveholders: impoverishment of during the war, 115, 212–13; opposition to secession of, 208–09

North Carolina: contributions to Confederacy of, 212; divisions within, 213–14; wartime relief programs in, 213

Northern peace party, 120, 124

Norwood, James, 183–84

Norwood, Joe, 21, 53, 105, 116, 120, 126, 137, 164

Norwood, Laura. *See* Lenoir, Laura

Norwood, Laura (Walter's niece), 69–70

Norwood, Louise, 70, 100

Norwood, Robina, 57

Norwood, Selina, 138, 198

Norwood, Thomas, 11, 93–94, 96, 113–15, 129; hatred of Yankees, 131; hunts for deserters, 120, 124; on soldiers' opposition to the war, 130–31, 212

Old South, in Lost Cause
mythology, 7–8, 225, 227
Outliers, 115, 133

Patterson, Rufus Lenoir, 145, 214
Patton, J. W., 148
Peace movement in North
Carolina, 121–22, 124, 135–36
Pickens, Israel, 19
Pickett's charge, 2
Polly, a slave, 98, 104, 152
Poor whites, 56, 103, 123, 147,
150, 153–54, 169, 182; role of
in Reconstruction, 213–15
Pope, John B., 77, 80, 85
Port Royal, Union capture of,
58, 60
Promissory notes, role in
Southern economy, 23, 59

Racial attitudes, of Southern
whites, 143–44, 151, 153–54,
170–71, 213
Railroads, and opening up of
western North Carolina,
187, 193
Reagan, James, 131
Reagan, Julia, 154
Reconstruction, 167–68,
213–15. *See also* Fourteenth
Amendment and Republican
party
Reese, David, 31

Religion, and the Lost Cause, 3–4
Republican party, 125, 208; and
election of 1876, 184; during
secession crisis, 48–49; in
postwar North Carolina, 167,
169–70, 173–76, 178–79, 214;
role in Reconstruction, 146,
160, 214
Richey, Reverend, 94
Rural poor, and the Lenoirs,
42–43

Secession, 6–8, 42–43; and
vindication of slavery, 219;
divisions over in South, 206–09,
220–21; in Lower South,
46–49; response in North
Carolina, 46. *See also* Southern
Unionists and Upper South
Secessionists, in Reconstruction,
170
Seward, William H., 51
Shaffner, Dr. John F., 90–92
Sherman, William Tecumseh, 133
Shull, Phillip, 168
Shulls Mill, 190, 197–98; Walter's
home at, 177, 186
Slaveholders: reaction to freeing
of slaves, 142–44, n. 165;
support for secession, 8, 208,
220
Slavery: and Walter's dread of
indebtedness, 184; defense
of, 149, 204, 220; in Cult of

the Lost Cause, 8; role of in secession, 8, 48, 149, 207–08, 220, 226; white attitudes on, 8, 148

Slaves: and the Lenoir family, 15–16, 18–20, 22, 24–25, 27, 29–30, 148; assist Yankee raiders, 138; attitudes toward work, 29; during Civil War, 6, 53, 60; freeing of during the war, 117–19, 137; marginally profitable at Fort Defiance, 25, 37–38, 144, 205; marriage ceremony of, 112–13; sale of by Lenoirs, 30, 38, 205; sold out of Upper South, 207; use of as Union troops,117–18, 210; walk off after the war, 152; wartime prices of, 65, 74, 103–04

Smith, Kirby, 75

South Carolina, takes the lead in secession, 46–48, 207

Southern elites: efforts to undermine Republican rule, 170, 174–75; minority of join the Republican party, 169; postwar fears of, 147, 214–15; promote the Lost Cause, 213; regain power in North Carolina, 184; reunited by defeat in Civil War, 217; support for secession, 211

Southern nationalism: as a product of the Civil War, 161; debate over, 210–11; distinct from Southern patriotism, 222

Southern Unionists, 101, 113, 115, 133, 168; and land confiscation, 158; in secession crisis, 10, 47, 49, 51, 207–09, 214, 220–21; reprisals against secessionists, 138, 141, 146; role in Reconstruction, 169–70; targeted by Klan, 179

Southern white identity, and Civil War, 13, 218–20. *See also* Lost Cause

Southern white women: commitment to Confederacy, 69; turn against the war, 115, 136

Southern whites: as a wronged people, 215; reaction to defeat in Civil War, 12

Sparks, Milton, 56

Sprinkle, Obadiah, 56

St. Domingue, slave revolt on, 118

Steele, Walter, 170

Stoneman's Raid, 136–38

Swain, David, 34

Thirty–Seventh North Carolina Regiment, 75, 81, n. 107, 113, 130, 212; opposition to war in, 130–31

Tobacco, postwar expansion of, 185–86

Tories. *See* Southern Unionists
Tourism, in western North
    Carolina, 193
Twenty Negro law, 211–12
Twenty-Fifth North Carolina
    Regiment, 54, 57, 63–64

Union raids, 105, 126–27,
    135–37, 141
Union soldiers, depicted as
    criminals, 69–70
United Confederate Veterans, 4
United Daughters of the
    Confederacy, 4
University of North Carolina,
    16, 27, 33–34, 219
Upper South: in contrast to
    Lower South, 7–8, 207–08;
    initially rejects secession,
    48–50; secession in, 51–52,
    206–09, 220–21; slaveholders
    in support secession, 149
Uriah, a slave, 61, 110, 112, 133

Vance, Zebulon B.: as wartime
    governor, 123, 130–31, 213;
    during secession crisis, 47–49,
    51, 207; elected governor after
    the war, 184, 215; on lack of
    popular support for the war, 211
Vance's Legion, 68, 71–72, 75

Walker, Peter, 217
Washington Peace Conference, 50
Watauga County: bushwackers in,
    120; landholdings of Walter in,
    168, 171–72, 177–78, 180, 186
Weaver, William, 81–83
Welsh, Lewis, 112
Whig party, 7–8, 47, 208–09
White labor, views of in postwar
    South, 151–55
White supremacy, calls for
    restoration of, 174, 184, 215
White tenants: and the Lenoirs,
    18, 20, 26–27, 30–32, 111, 144,
    177, 181, 197, 205–06; during
    the war, 67; in prewar South,
    206
White trash. *See* Poor whites
Wilkes County: lack of
    enthusiasm for the war,
    55–56; opponents of war in,
    115; plagued by robbers, 134.
    See also Stoneman's Raid
Worth, Jonathan, 145, 221
Wounds in Civil War, nature of, 91